Bad
Habits

ALSO BY

JENNY McCARTHY

Love, Lust & Faking It

Healing and Preventing Autism

Mother Warriors

Louder than Words

Life Laughs

Baby Laughs

Belly Laughs

Bad Habits

Confessions of a
Recovering Catholic

JENNY
McCARTHY

HYPERION

NEW YORK

Grateful acknowledgment is made to the following for permission to reproduce illustrations in the text: pages 6, 10, 24, 33, 42, 50, 55, 78, 93, 110, 118, 172, 214: photographs courtesy of Jenny McCarthy. Page 144: photograph courtesy of Ron Galella/Ron Galella Collection/ Getty Images. Page 163: photograph © Playboy. Page 180: photograph courtesy of Alberto E. Rodriguez/Getty Images Entertainment/Getty Images. Page 206: photograph © Adam Bouska.

Hyperion
Hachette Book Group
237 Park Avenue
New York, NY 10017

www.HachetteBookGroup.com

Printed in the United States of America

RRD-C

Originally published in hardcover by Hyperion as *Bad Habits: Confessions of a Recovering Catholic*

Book design by Karen Minster

First trade edition: January 2014
10 9 8 7 6 5 4 3 2 1

Hyperion is a division of Hachette Book Group

The Hachette Speakers Bureau provides a wide range of authors for speaking events. To find out more, go to www.hachettespeakersbureau.com or call (866) 376-6591.

The publisher is not responsible for websites (or their content) that are not owned by the publisher.

The Library of Congress cataloged the hardcover edition as follows:

McCarthy, Jenny.
   Bad habits: confessions of a recovering Catholic/Jenny McCarthy.— 1st ed.
     p. cm.
   ISBN 978-1-4013-2465-0
   1. McCarthy, Jenny, 1972—Childhood and youth. 2. Catholic children—Illinois—Chicago—Biography. 3. Girls—Illinois—Chicago—Biography. 4 Catholics—Illinois—Chicago—Biography. 5. Catholics—Illinois—Chicago—Social life and customs. 6. Chicago (Ill.)—Biography. 7. Chicago (Ill.)— Social life and customs. 8. Catholics—Humor. I. Title.
   F548.9.C3M33 2012
   977.3'11092—dc23

2012015573

ISBN 978-1-4013-1262-6 (pbk.)

For Mom and Dad

Not sure if God chose you to be my parents or
I chose you, but I will be eternally grateful for the gift
of love and faith you instilled in my sisters and me.
Well . . . JoJo could use a little more help, but for the
most part I think you both did an amazing job.

CONTENTS

Bad
Habits

I Knew I Should Have Worn Underwear to Church

L ord, You are holy indeed, the fountain of all holiness . . ."

Father Colin conducted the service in his usual mono-tone delivery. He was middle-aged and portly with jiggly jowls. He always wore humongous glasses and bore a strong re-semblance to Peter Griffin from *Family Guy*.

"Let Your spirit come upon these gifts to make them holy so that they may become . . ."

Squeak, squeak.

Father Colin stopped mid-prayer as the parishioners looked around. He needn't look at the three altar boys who always stood behind him like the three amigos (except they weren't friends), be-cause they were ass-kissers and not at all mischievous. They were in their early teens, and didn't even let out an occasional snicker at deaf Mrs. Connors and her loud farts that managed to slip out at the quietest of times.

Squeak, squeak.

Father Colin started to look agitated. He took one more scan of the room before continuing.

". . . so that they may become for us the body and blood of our Lord Jesus . . ."

Squeak, squeak.

Father Colin's head snapped up, trying to catch the little pissant making the disturbing noise that kept interrupting his 157,000th Mass service.

Squeak, squeak.

"What *is* that noise?" Father Colin shouted.

Once again, all the parishioners looked around at each other as if to say, "It's not coming from me."

I was six years old and sitting with my mom and dad, older sister Lynette, and younger sisters JoJo and Amy. My mother was a hairdresser, so she made sure all of her daughters were coiffed perfectly. We were always dressed beautifully, even though we were poor as shit. We looked liked the kids from the show *Toddlers & Tiaras*.

Squeak, squeak.

The parishioners began looking at our section. My mother turned around to stare at the pew behind us, trying to deflect some of the stares we were getting.

My mother's expression changed as she spotted her worst enemy. Almost like when Jerry Seinfeld would see Newman.

My mom's enemy was named Janet Baruch.

The Baruch family lived on the same street as us, but they had six children. Janet would always try to outdo my mother in everything—having the most plastic fake-animal decorations on her lawn; donating more time to charities; even having two more children than my mom.

My mom and Janet stared at each other with an intense gaze

that you usually see only at the beginning of a UFC fight. It was the look my mom had the time she went over to Janet's and kicked over her fake-duck family, the newest addition to her creepy lawn.

Janet said, "I think the noise is coming from one of your children, Linda."

Now, let me tell you something about my mother. She is one of the most wonderful, loving, caring, sweet people you will ever meet—unless you cross her family.

My mother used her infamous fake smile while talking through clenched teeth to reply. "No, Janet. I'm pretty sure it's coming from your pew. And speaking of pew, I think your baby could use a diaper change."

My mom sat back with pursed lips, pleased with her response.

Squeak, squeak.

Father Colin threw his hands up in the air and shouted, "Okay, I'm sure most of you don't want to be here all day, so whoever is making that noise, please stop."

My dad did a once-over at all of us. He always had that Irish, blue-collar, exhausted look and liked to turn a blind eye to controversy. I smiled sweetly to reassure him of my innocence, as did Lynette. My two other sisters, Amy and JoJo, were too young to possibly create this bizarre sound, so my dad leaned back and his eyes began to flutter and close as he fell back asleep. This was Dad's usual nap time. A few other people were dozing off too, so it appeared that they were also safe from being labeled as the holy squeaker.

Lynette leaned over to me and said, "I think it's coming from Greg."

Our neighbors, the Baruchs, were sitting right behind us. Greg Baruch, the son, was the same age as I was and was an evil little prick.

One time, Greg peed inside my Baby Alive doll after I left it in our backyard. He told me about it two days later—after I had already resumed playing with her. Imagine my horror when real pee came out of my doll's vagina hole! I thought she was possessed. I screamed and ran inside the house to tell my mom, who then stormed over to the Baruchs.

Janet came out and accused my mother of lying about her precious Greg. A screaming match followed as she adamantly defended that Greg "would do no such thing." I looked upstairs to his bedroom window and saw the asshole laughing. Later that month when I heard my parents talking after I was "asleep," they made reference to my dad getting revenge.

I can only imagine where my dad might have unloaded his bladder.

Meanwhile, in church, I whispered back to Lynette, "Yeah, I think it's Greg too."

Then Lynette leaned over to my mother and said, "Ma, the sound is coming from Greg."

My mother quickly turned around and proudly whispered, "Janet, my daughter just told me that the squeak is coming from Greg, not my kids, so don't be so quick to judge. Remember Matthew 7:1: 'Do not judge, or you too will be judged.'"

Janet leaned in ready to counterattack. "First of all, it's 'Judge not, lest ye be judged.' Don't butcher the Bible—and Greg is not making that noise."

Squeak, squeak.

My mom and Janet both whipped their heads in their kids' direction. I immediately looked at Greg and pointed to him. Janet violently tugged Greg's ear and loudly whispered into it, "I will beat your ass raw if that sound is coming from you." I heard him whimper, and for a moment I felt redemption for the doll urination act.

The Mass continued.

It was like the scene from *Ferris Bueller's Day Off* when the dull teacher keeps saying, "Bueller . . . Bueller . . . Bueller . . . Bueller," in his flat voice while the class is half asleep. I think some parishioners were actually drooling.

Squeak, squeaaaaaak!

Not anymore. Everyone inside the church jolted and suddenly became alert with this last squeak.

Then came another *sque—*, which was abruptly stopped by a church usher grabbing me.

"It's coming from her," he pointed dramatically, as if he had caught a thief stealing a precious jewel.

The entire church gasped: How could such an adorable, innocent-looking blond girl in a fluffy pink dress be the squeaker? I looked over at my mom. She turned pale and mumbled softly, "What in the heck?"

Even at this young age, I remembered that honesty is always the best policy, so I said, "I like the noise my butt makes on the pew when I don't wear underwear." Then I proceeded to illustrate to everyone that I was telling the truth by lifting up my dress as I stood up on the bench and did a spin, just like a pageant girl would do, except only mine flashed my bum cheeks.

Mom couldn't pull me back down fast enough as I fell on my tush with a thud.

As my mother dragged us out of church that day, a little piece of her died. This was the beginning of Jenny testing her faith and patience. It was also the beginning of my love of not wearing underwear.

me in church

2

The Age of Innocence

As a little girl, I spent a lot of time staring up at the sky. I felt an amazing connection to it. It felt like home to me. I can still remember the warm breeze that would glide across my face as my eyes wondrously gazed up to the heavens.

I think I was only about five or six years old during this time. I hadn't gone to school yet to learn how to be a Catholic, so all I had was my reliance on an innate knowledge in my soul that God was glorious. God was real.

In my house, I would visit the bathroom regularly to have meetings with my guardian angels. I would sit on the floor and discuss important things with them for hours. This was until my mom eventually pulled me out because to her, I was just talking to the walls. I would stare into the mirror (not because I was unusually vain but because it was fascinating). I was intrigued that a mirror was an instant telling of who we are. Beyond just the reflection. I would stare intently at myself to try to see through my young soul and understand what it meant to be me in this world.

The biggest issue I had at that age was whether dinner would be yummy that night. I walked around free of concern and with love in my heart. I hadn't yet been programmed to worry about Satan, money, or anything else.

I realize now that the more catechism I had through the years, the less connected to the heavens I felt. The love in my heart morphed into fear. To be told stories at such a young age about the wrath of God doing dreadful things like floods and famine made staring at the sky go from love to worry.

On walks home from school, I would keep my head down because I felt like God was always watching me from a soft, cotton candy–textured cloud. Learning that God can really get pissed off and do bad things to us on Earth paralyzed me with fear.

Then, as if that weren't enough, I learned about Hell. I was told that Hell is the place where sinners go to spend a horrific eternity in torture and despair. As further descriptions of Hell were taught, I felt my heart breaking. The beautiful world that I used to float around in as a little girl became dark and terrifying.

What if I wasn't good enough to make it to Heaven? The little girl I stared at in the mirror suddenly had more questions that needed answering because the world had become more confusing.

To make matters even worse, I was told a demon named Satan used temptations on Earth to bring us to his fiery pit. As you will read in future chapters, this caused irreparable damage to my childhood.

Being taught by nuns was no help either. I looked at them as if they were psychically connected to God, so I initially believed everything they said. They also worked hard to constantly remind us about Hell in order to help us remain good.

"Don't forget, kids, if you break a commandment, you will burn in a fiery pit for all eternity. Now go have a great day!"

Looking at Hell now from a grown-up perspective, I can't think of a better way to get people to follow rules. All you have to do is scare the shit out of them. I'll have to try that with my son, Evan, sometime and see how well it works.

"Evan, if you don't clean your room, I'm afraid you're going to burn in Hell forever."

I bet his room would be cleaner than a bar of soap.

Sister Jenny

I was seven years old when I told my mother my dream of becoming a nun. She couldn't have been more proud. To me, it seemed like an obvious profession. I loved the idea of being a teacher, and if I got a straight ticket to Heaven by putting a habit on, why in the heck would anyone not want to be a nun? It seemed so logical. The fear of going to Hell was constantly on my mind. I became extremely paranoid and was scared to do anything that could possibly alter my final destination—Heaven.

The nuns made themselves look like Mother Mary, who was so beautiful to me. I would wrap my head up in a towel, put a crucifix on, and glide around the house blessing my family. My mom told me that nuns hear a voice from God telling them to become nuns, and I desperately awaited those words from God.

In these early years, when I went to school, I would kiss the nuns' holy butts. I wanted to be part of their sorority and tried to be teacher's pet.

My mom used to do their hair in the convent, so one day she decided to take me with her.

Walking into a convent is pretty much like walking into the

meat department at a grocery store—cold and a bit stinky. My mom rang a little bell. What happened next will haunt me forever.

Around the corner came three of the nuns from my school without their habits on and dressed in normal clothes! This was devastating to my seven-year-old psyche. My young brain couldn't handle seeing these nuns gallivanting around in their casual attire and intermingling with us as everyday humans. They were superior to us. These women were married to God, but now one of them was wearing a Freddie Mercury T-shirt. Did they not know that he was flaming gay? Well, I guess that was a common misconception at the time. But did the nuns lead a secret life that the rest of us weren't allowed to discover? I felt betrayed for being in the dark, but I was also more intrigued than ever. I wanted to know more about their double life, but in that moment, it was too much to take in, and really, I just wanted to run and hide. The confusion overwhelmed me so I did what any seven-year-old would do. I burst into tears. Unfortunately, this only drew more attention and made them all run toward me.

"What's wrong, little angel?" they asked so sweetly.

"You look scary. You don't look like you do at school," I responded in horror as I hid behind my mother's leg.

"Well, we don't wear our habits all day long."

What the heck? Were they like uniforms? I couldn't imagine the nuns wearing anything else, as if the habits were stitched to their bodies.

As their faces drew in closer to mine to comfort me, I was also amazed by their facial hair. I thought, *Why do they have beards? Are they men?*

My mother tried to do the clever trick that moms do when their child might be behaving rudely. She gave me giant saucer eyes that beamed an invisible laser into my soul to shut me up.

I then followed my mom down a corridor. As we passed the rooms, I was able to catch a glimpse into the life of a nun. Many were reading or knitting. It was also painfully quiet—the kind of quiet that makes your ears ring. It was like the convent was set at the right frequency for everyone to always tune in to the God channel without interference.

Finally, we made it to a large room where my mom began to set up her hair stuff. I was doing that thing kids do where every step your mom tries to take, you block it and get in the way.

"Jenny, you need to sit down," Mom said. "Or go walk around and talk to some of the nuns."

"*No!*" I yelled.

"Okay, fine then. Just sit in that chair and sit still."

I walked over to the chair she was pointing to, clutching my Cabbage Patch doll, and sat down. More nuns started entering and mingling about. I heard them talking about some other members of the church. "So-and-so is such an alcoholic," they would mumble. Later on in life, I struggled with the term "alcoholic." Considering I'm Irish Catholic, it seemed like every other person was an alcoholic. From my young perspective, it just seemed like "alcoholic" was a name given to the dads who yelled louder than the other drunks.

As I sat there eavesdropping and combing my Cabbage Patch doll's hair, a nun came and sat next to me. "What's your baby's name?"

"Well, her birth certificate said Mandy, but I changed it to Sarah."

The nun chuckled. "I bet you're going to be a great mom when you grow up."

"Yes, and I'm gonna be a great nun, like you."

The nun looked perplexed (rightfully so) and said, "Well, in order to be a nun, you have to make a promise to God and not have any children."

My heart started beating quickly. What was this crazy nun saying to me?

I responded, "I have to be a mom, a nun, and a teacher. That's what I'm going to be."

The nun replied, "Okay, first tell me why you want to be a nun."

"Because you go straight to Heaven."

Again, she giggled. "Just because you are a nun doesn't mean you go straight to Heaven."

This nun was really raining on my parade. First she tells me I can't have a baby and then she tells me being a nun isn't a straight ticket to Heaven.

"Why do you want to be a teacher?" she asked.

"Because I love helping and being the leader. And if I'm a nun, I get paid for being a teacher and being close to God."

"We don't get paid to teach. We do it for the love of the parish and the children."

If I had been older I would have yelled, "OMG, are you crazy? You're telling me I can't be a mom, I don't get a guarantee into Heaven, and I make no money?"

But instead of saying that, I smiled sweetly, rose from my chair, walked over to my mom, and tugged on her nylons.

"Mom!"

"What is it?"

"I think I'm going to take my chances with Hell and be Wonder Woman instead."

I wore a Wonder Woman costume for the next eight years. I may not have become a nun, but looking up to an empowered woman such as Wonder Woman made little Jenny believe that even though you don't marry God like the nuns do, girls can use their power to fight for truth and look damn good in a push-up bra while doing it.

4

I Want to Be a Jew!

I want to be a Jew!" I exclaimed to Sister Grace Downey, my strict third-grade teacher.

"What? Why in the world would you say that?" she snapped back.

I remember her mustache glistening under the light with a vengeance. She had tits the size of pomelos. She was a no-nonsense, control-top pantyhose–wearing, stiff-upper-hairy-lipped woman who had lived through the Great Depression. Her cold demeanor made it difficult to know if she ever truly survived it. I don't think Sister Grace Downey had had a day of fun in her entire adult life.

This hardened woman was supposed to be my role model and my confidante. She scared the hell out of me.

I confronted her just three months before my first Holy Communion.

Maybe this was a big mistake, but there were questions weighing heavily on my mind and it was time to get them off my chest.

I logically explained, "Jesus was right about everything. We're supposed to be just like him and believe everything he said. So why would Jesus pick the wrong religion? He is a Jew! Seems like we should all be Jewish."

Sister Grace Downey took a deep breath and explained to innocent little Jenny that Jews were responsible for slaughtering Jesus. She tried to convince me that the Jews did not believe that Jesus was the Son of God.

To which little Jenny responded, "Well, maybe Jewish people think he's just like us. Didn't you say that we are all the sons and daughters of God? Maybe he's not an only child after all. Maybe I'm his sister. Maybe Fonzie is his uncle."

I'll never forget the distraught look on Sister Grace Downey's face. I was literally saved by the bell because I swear to God that nun was so close to opening the window and hanging me by my feet.

The next week, in religion class, she casually explained that unbaptized babies who died unexpectedly would not go to Heaven.

"Where do they go?" I asked nervously.

"Purgatory or Limbo," she replied as if she were reading the daily offerings of a lunch menu. "It's a place where souls float around and are stuck. A world between Heaven and Hell."

Sister Grace Downey made it sound like souls were stuck like an infinity of Pac-Man ghosts bumping into each other for all eternity.

"How do you know if Limbo is a real place?" I asked.

Sister Grace Downey quickly responded, "Because the Church said so."

I continued to do what I always do best, which is question things that don't make sense. I wasn't convinced by her answer, and my curiosity needed to be satisfied. I was willing to challenge Sister

Grace Downey to uncover the truth even if it meant sacrificing my lunch hour in detention with the old hag.

"Has somebody from the Church been in Limbo before? Has someone said that they went there and saw dead babies floating around? That doesn't seem fair. That seems like God is a mean God. It's not the babies' fault they didn't get baptized. Why should they be punished? Shouldn't the parents take the blame for that one? Isn't there foster care in Heaven for babies born into bad families? Doesn't that make God a big jerk if He likes to torture innocent little babies?"

Sister Grace Downey slammed her Bible on my desk and demanded that I stop asking questions because I was confusing the class. I listened because her mustache was getting sweaty and her hands were shaking.

Was I responsible for giving her a violent hot flash? I never did well with unanswered questions, so I decided to bombard any adult I came across after school to try to help me.

As I did, I received even more bad news.

I learned that Catholics who haven't gone to confession and accidentally die with a sin on their soul go straight to Hell. That's right, Hell. Even if they are good people! Did this mean that God was a sadist? What if Heaven is just a final destination where God uses us as little playthings He brainwashes into having Stockholm syndrome?

I often caught myself daydreaming in class if Sister Grace Downey didn't catch me first. I needed time to absorb everything and make sense of it all, but it was hard to sift through the information I was being fed in order to uncover the truth.

I often wondered if I would ever really know.

I was only nine years old when I started to become overwhelmed with the fear of dying with a sin on my soul. So I started to go to confession once a week.

"Forgive me, Father, for I have sinned," I would plead to our local parish priest, Father Bill, who was a raging alcoholic.

"What now, Jenny?" he would slur.

"I have not loved God as I should because . . . I committed adultery."

"What?" Father Bill said with concern.

"I committed adultery. I tried to come yesterday, but you were closed."

"How old are you, Jenny?" he slurred.

"I'm nine," I said proudly.

He continued: "Jenny, what do you think adultery means?"

I explained that adultery meant saying swear words like "shit," "bitch," "damn," and "crap."

"That's not what it means, Jenny."

"What does it mean?"

Silence came from Father Bill. I thought he had fallen asleep. So I squinted through the confessional screen to make sure he was still breathing. I knew he was still alive from the smell of whiskey that came blasting my way as he uttered his response. "It's when two people . . . um . . . it's if your mom or dad . . . um, well . . . You don't have to worry about this one. Just ignore it."

I couldn't have been more perplexed. "What? How am I supposed to ignore it? What if I break it? I'll burn in Hell for all eternity or worse. I could float around with dead babies!"

"What?"

"Well, it doesn't make any sense. We are supposed to follow these commandments, but you won't explain what it means. How am I supposed to avoid going to Hell if you won't explain the rules of how to stay out?"

"Go in peace, Jenny."

With that, the screen door shut and I sat alone in the confessional wondering if I would accidentally commit this unknown adultery in the next few days.

When I got to school the next day, I asked Sister Grace Downey about confession. I raised my hand.

"What now, Jenny?" Sister Grace Downey said.

"So answer me this. We will burn in Hell if we don't confess all of our sins before we die, right?"

"That's correct," she replied.

I continued. "Okay, but what if you commit a sin and then run to church, but they're closed and then you die? Does God know that you tried to confess your sins so you should get a free pass considering it's the church's fault they were closed?"

I could tell Sister Grace Downey hated me.

The questions I asked were logical, but not necessarily in the Church's guidebook.

"If you go to confession at least once a week, I'm sure God will take that into consideration. Does that answer your question?"

I didn't like her response and made her aware of it. "It doesn't sound like you're sure about that. It sounds like you're guessing.

This is a big deal, not something you should be guessing. We're talking about melting in a fire pit for an eternity here."

She fired back, "Then you will probably go to Limbo."

"What?!" I screamed. I would rather burn in flames than see dead babies floating around for all eternity!"

Let me explain something about myself at this age. I was a good student and a great daughter because I was a rule follower. (Again, only at this age.) If you set boundaries, I obeyed them without a problem. So all you needed to do was tell me exactly what they were and I would follow them.

The problem I had with understanding Catholicism was that it seemed like there were loopholes everywhere. In my young brain, I couldn't quite grasp how there could be any loopholes with the very strict set of rules they gave us. It really confused me. I began to wonder how I could follow these rules when I didn't even know what they truly meant.

Sister Grace Downey said, "Jenny, if you are that worried about dying with sins on your soul, go buy a scapular."

"What's a scapular?" I said with hope.

"A scapular is a string necklace that has a picture of the Stations of the Cross on them." (A picture of Jesus dying, basically.)

"What will that do?" I asked.

She replied, "It will protect you from going to Hell if you die with a sin on your soul. It costs about ten to fifteen dollars."

"What?" I exclaimed. "So all I need to do is pay fifteen dollars and I get to go to Heaven?"

I couldn't have run out of school fast enough to beg my mom to take me to the religious store to get me a scapular. I remember picking out the most expensive one. It was nineteen dollars. I figured that God would appreciate the fact that I cared enough to pay for the most luxurious scapular. I thought the more money, the more sins I could pile up on it and everything would be okay.

This theory is similar to the concept of a computer hard drive that holds sins.

I'm not going to lie that while I was digging the cash out of my pocket to pay for the damn thing, I already had a few sins in mind I was really excited about committing.

Looking back, I must say it's one of the greatest loopholes the Church came up with—and not to mention one of the most profitable. I did not go a day without my scapular on. I was going to make every effort to stay out of Limbo, and wearing that cloth necklace, which eventually infected my skin from wearing it so long, seemed totally worth it.

Just this year I was scrolling through the AOL news page and saw a headline that made me fall off my chair. The Catholic Church announced that it had decided Limbo does not exist. It never existed.

I couldn't believe it. I was in shock.

How could they just change the rules like that? Did everyone sin so badly that there was a unanimous vote? Was the entire Catholic Church a group of sinners who needed to repent? Was this the art of positive thinking or did God create a divine intervention and whisper to them in a dream, "Hey, idiots, limbo is just a game that swingers play."

Who gave them the authority to suddenly eliminate the whole Limbo theory? This made no sense to me.

I always thought all these rules came from God, so how in the heck was the Church allowed to change such a huge belief it had brainwashed us into believing? Does it know the amount of endless suffering I endured and the sleepless nights I stayed up praying rosaries for all the dead baby souls throughout my adolescence?

And what is the verdict on masturbation? Does God mind? Does He want us to? I can't tell you how many recurring nightmares I have had of me alone with my defunct vibrator floating around Limbo forever.

I still have so many questions left unanswered.

How many other things has the Church changed its rules on since I've been to school? How many beliefs do I still walk around with that are affecting my everyday life that the Church has now overturned? I guess I am always on a journey to find out.

5

I'm Totally Possessed by the Devil, Like Totally

W ant to scare your children forever? If so, rent the movie *The Exorcist*.

In third grade, I had my first Holy Communion. I felt more holy than I'd ever felt because I got to eat the sacred body and drink the blood of Christ. I had no idea what that meant, but since all the adults got to do it, I thought I was that much closer to God.

My mom and dad threw a grand party for me that night. My entire family attended as well as my dad's friend George, who welcomed any occasion as an excuse to drink.

Every time an aunt or uncle walked in with a card for me, I ran into my bedroom, opened it, and counted the money. I was always very good at saving. By the time the last guest showed up, I had made a whopping one hundred dollars. Eating Jesus's body was really lucrative. I knew exactly what I was going to buy too—more Cabbage Patch dolls.

After dinner, my uncle shouted that *The Exorcist* was going to be on TV. I remember a loud rumble from the kitchen as my relatives raced to the living room like they were rushing to the scene of a car accident.

So like any curious kid, I ran into the TV room with my sisters and cousins. My entire family was debating whether we should be allowed to watch the movie. Some thought it was too extreme. Others thought it would be a good reminder that you need faith to fight the dark side. My uncle didn't seem to care either way as long as the decision meant he could quickly get back to the kitchen to finish the glass of brandy he'd left there. Many sets of eyes were locked to the television as though they were stuck in a hypnotic trance. I didn't understand how a movie could have such a polarizing effect on people. Now I do.

It was decided that we could watch the movie while George pulled our parents into the other room to play poker. After all, movies are great babysitters, as we moms know. Plus it was the only channel that came in clear after three men fussed around trying to adjust the rabbit ears for fifteen minutes.

"*Exorcist* it is," George said as he summoned the adults into the kitchen.

So all the kids huddled on the couch. I made sure JoJo sat next to me. We demon fighters needed to stick together.

As the movie played, terror ran through my blood. I was already terrified of our basement, and now I had a visual for what happens to a young girl when she becomes possessed by the devil. She pukes green, her head spins around, and her voice sounds like a demon.

My young brain immediately thought, *This is totally going to happen to me. The demons know I'm not strong and will take over my body any second.*

When the movie was finished, my cousins and I sat in silence. We couldn't speak.

I looked over at JoJo and saw she was catatonic.

"JoJo? JoJo, are you okay?" I asked.

"Jknasbdbkneiu," she slurred.

We were totally screwed.

We all quietly got up and walked into the room where our parents were playing poker. We stood there just staring at them like zombies. They began staring back at us. No one was talking. My cousins and I were the wildest group of kids at these parties, but now, after watching this movie, it looked like we'd had lobotomies.

"You kids okay?"

Again, we stood there in silence.

Did they have any idea of the emotional scars they'd just given us? We would have been better off getting whipped with belts than having to endure a lifetime of that visual.

"No, I don't think we're okay. I'm pretty sure the devil is coming for my body, and probably JoJo's too."

Then JoJo started screaming as if she were being stabbed to death, which made all of us scream. We then proceeded to run upstairs to my bedroom and huddle in a corner. A few of my cousins were crying.

I tried to console them. "You guys have nothing to worry about. The devil is, for sure, coming to get me."

"So he's not coming for me?" JoJo said, relieved as she wiped away her tears.

"I think he wants my soul," I replied. "But I'm not going alone, so you have to get possessed with me."

Then JoJo started screaming and crying again, which made all of us start screaming and crying again. Then we heard footsteps in the hallway and we immediately became quiet.

"Oh no, it's Satan. He's here," I said. "Let me just get it over with. Okay, Satan, just do it already!" I stood up and squeezed my eyes tight.

My uncle opened the door. We all breathed a sigh of relief.

"Get your butts downstairs," he said. "No one is getting possessed, you little shit stains." Maybe he didn't say exactly that, but he had a very stern tone of voice and I suspect it was because he had been interrupted from his brandy once again.

With that, we were all forced to get out of our protective corner and go downstairs.

None of us spoke for the remainder of the night. How could we? We were absolutely traumatized. The fear of Satan always looming made *The Exorcist* one of the best-kept secrets of the Catholic Church.

The days that followed haunted JoJo and me. It was as if we were on death row awaiting our painful demise. It would be a very long time before we would go to the basement to wash sheets again. For now, we just laid in pee all night long. We had so many pee-stained sheets that I wouldn't doubt if Mom went through a tub of bleach every month.

At school, I told some of my friends about our night watching *The Exorcist*. They told me the devil went by a common name in order to blend in with society. Lucifer was too obvious, so he chose the name Ben. If Ben shows up, it means Satan is near.

I ran home and told my mom about this. She laughed and told

me how ridiculous that was and said I needed to stop getting so worked up about everything.

Later that week, I wanted to go spend some of my Holy Communion money, so I asked my mom to take me shopping. Even at a young age, shopping really does take a girl's worries away.

I chose a beautiful new Cabbage Patch doll. This was my seventh one. My bedroom had started to look like Angelina Jolie's house. I had dolls from every ethnicity and I loved them all.

When I got home, all my sisters gathered around to watch me open my newest doll box. The excitement was like Charlie finding a golden ticket in a Wonka Bar. I pulled my fresh baby out of its box and we did what we always did—pull the pants down and make sure it had butt cheeks like the rest of the Cabbage Patch dolls.

Then I pulled out his birth certificate and saw the name: Ben.

"Oh my God!" I screamed, and frantically ran to my mom. "Satan is here! Damn it, Mom, Satan is here!" I cried, holding her leg.

"Jenny, what in God's name are you talking about?"

"My baby's name is Ben! His name is Ben! It's the devil, Mom. He's coming for me!"

"I knew I shouldn't have let you watch that movie. You need to calm the hell down, Jenny. You are not going to be possessed."

How could I believe any adults at this point? My friends at school obviously knew more than they did.

My next problem was figuring out how to get rid of Ben. I walked back upstairs and looked at Ben lying there on the floor. I picked him up slowly and walked into my backyard. I spun in circles, let go, and watched Ben/Satan fly into the air. I had no idea where he landed, but I was happy he was gone.

Ding dong.

"Hi, Linda, this doll just landed in our pool," our neighbor said to my mom. "I thought it must belong to one of your girls."

"Jenny!" my mom shouted.

Ben/Satan had returned to the house. I grabbed the doll and walked right out the back door. I moved quickly toward the alley, where we kept our garbage cans, while I recited the Our Father prayer. To me, reciting the Lord's Prayer was like using bug spray in the summertime. It was a repellent that worked and this bug needed to be squashed immediately.

I opened the heavy lid with my little arms and threw Ben/Satan in the trash, where he belonged. I stomped back into the house with high hopes that it was the last I would see or hear of Ben/Satan.

About a year later, my mom adopted a bunny for my sisters and me. Its former owners couldn't care for it anymore. We all decided on the name Zack. When the bunny got there, it was black and fluffy. We all attacked it like it was cotton candy.

The owners were saying their last good-byes and the woman turned around and said, "You'll be in good hands now, Ben."

"Take it back!" I shouted.

My mom caught on right away. "Jenny, stop that!" she yelled.

"No, Mom, it's you know who!"

The woman asked, "Who is you know who?"

My mom tried to cover it up with a giggle. "It's no one really," she said.

"Take it back," I shouted. "I don't want a devil bunny in our house!"

"I'm sorry, what?" said the lady.

"I'm talking about Satan. You just brought Satan into this house and I want you to take him back with you."

"That's enough, Jennifer," said my mom. "Go to your room."

"No, Mom. The bunny has to go. It's me or the bunny."

My sisters Amy and Lynette shouted, "Keep the bunny, Mom!"

I stormed upstairs and cried on my bed. Satan was getting closer to me, and my sisters didn't even care. My family kept the bunny because majority ruled. I would stare at him from far, far away. Everyone knew to keep him away from me because otherwise someone would suffer the wrath of my mighty little fists in their face.

JoJo, who pretty much did everything I did, stayed away from Ben/Satan/Zack too. She didn't want to take any chances of my being right, so we stuck together on this one.

About two years later, the bunny died. Needless to say, I did not attend the backyard funeral. I watched from my window as Dad dug a hole by the garden and placed the shoebox in there.

"I hope you're really dead, Ben," I said.

By the time high school came along, my fears of being possessed remained intact, but I talked about it less. I wanted to be cool, so I didn't let on to my obsessive-compulsive disorder about becoming possessed by the devil.

I was invited to a sleepover, and as usual we played the game Light as a Feather, Stiff as a Board. I'm grateful the Internet didn't exist back then, because God knows what we would have been doing on those sleepovers.

After that G-rated game, my friend Linney pulled out a Ouija board. "You guys want to try to summon a spirit?" she asked.

"Hell, no. No way. I get freaked out by that stuff," I said as cool as possible.

"Don't be a dork, Jenny. It's just stupid fun."

So I put on a brave face as we all sat around in a circle. We put our hands on the arrow and began moving it.

Linney did the commentating. "Are there any spirits here?"

Swish, swish went the arrow. It wasn't landing anywhere.

"Are you a child spirit?" said Erin.

Swish, swish went the arrow.

It landed on NO.

All the girls gasped.

"Are you guys moving this thing?" I asked.

"No, the spirit is moving it," said Erin.

"How old are you?" asked Linney.

Swish, swish.

The arrow went to NO.

"See, this is stupid. Let's stop. It's not even answering the questions correctly," I pleaded.

"What is your name?" asked Erin.

Swish, swish.

I shit you not that the arrow went to the letter *B*.

That's all I needed to see. I grabbed the board, ran out into the middle of the street, and threw the game as far as I could. I had never told my friends the Ben/Satan story, and I was thoroughly convinced that demons were still chasing me. I called my mom to pick me up and I went home.

There was also the time in college when a guy named Charles and I went to his place. As we stumbled into his bedroom to make out, his dog jumped on the bed.

"Ben, get down," he yelled.

I was running down the street before Charles turned back around to kiss me.

To this day, I still get freaked out by the name Ben. It's the dumbest thing ever, but you will never see me watch a Ben Stiller movie or date anyone named Ben.

I was often taunted by Michael Jackson's song . . . you guessed it . . . "Ben"—and especially during the holidays.

Now don't get any bright ideas at an autograph signing and bring me a Cabbage Patch doll named Ben. JoJo and I would have to do to you what we did to the bunny.

Just kidding.

me

gang of cousins

6

Jenny's First Fall from Grace

I was about nine years old when my mom showed me a picture of Satan in a religious book. It was the first time I had a visual of what this infamous demon that everyone seemed to be frightened of looked like.

He was green with horns and looked quite comfortable standing in a fire pit that seemed to melt the skin of only the evildoers around him. I trembled at the sight of him. I was surprised that he didn't match the red-horned man I saw on Halloween. When I inquired how Satan came to be, my mom explained that he was a fallen angel.

I visualized this angel accidentally slipping on a stair in Heaven and falling miles to Hell. Because I wasn't taught in detail about his fall from grace, I spent the next few years terrified of stairs. I would hold on for dear life thinking that if I fell, I too would become "a Satan."

What Catholicism—or any religion for that matter—doesn't realize is that children's minds will go to great lengths to try to understand what they are being taught, even when taught poorly. Since most of the Bible is metaphorical, it should be taught as such.

There were just too many questions unanswered and it seemed as though there was nobody willing to listen.

Don't get me wrong. I loved being a part of the Church. I loved how it gave a real sense of community and belonging. I have fond memories of attending our church bazaars and bake sales to help raise money for poor families like my own that were struggling to make ends meet.

Even though we were one of the poorest families at our church, my mother refused to accept handouts. She was simply too proud. We barely scraped by at times, but my mom wouldn't allow us to admit defeat. This caused a lot of frustration for me growing up, but it also made me admire my parents' strong work ethic and determination to persevere despite any obstacle thrown our way.

My sister JoJo and I were very close growing up, mainly because we both shared a fear of Satan and would not leave each other's side in the off chance that he would try to steal our souls. We had each other's backs so much so that she never slept a day in her own room. I had a twin bed, and after my parents went to sleep, she would crawl into it. Then we would pull out our Mother Mary statue, St. Joseph statue, Jesus statue, and four rosaries and make them into a wall around our bodies to protect us from any looming demons. Our nightly talk was about what we would do if Satan walked into the room. We had plans. Big ones. I would throw my Jesus statue at Satan and JoJo would drown him in holy water that we stole from the church in hopes of melting him like the witch in *The Wizard of Oz*.

This behavior could largely be the reason why JoJo and I were both bed wetters until we were ten years old. Every night, without fail, JoJo and I woke up in pee. Because we both knew we wet the bed, we stopped blaming each other.

It finally got to the point that my mother said that if either of us peed anymore, she would put us in diapers. The thought of that was traumatizing. We had to come up with yet another master plan; this time to cover our bladder handicap from our mom.

Come two A.M., one of us would usually wake up soaked and then shake the other one to get up. Then JoJo and I would tiptoe from our bedroom down into the basement to wash and dry the sheets and bring them back up.

The problem was that the basement is where the devil hangs out. So JoJo and I would strip the sheets off the bed and then put all of our rosaries around our necks until we looked like Mr. T or, for all you youngsters out there, Flavor Flav.

Once we were heavily weighed down with prayer beads, we would slowly open the basement door. There was always a creepy, musty, cold breeze that would flow toward us when we opened the door. Usually, we would nudge each other and fight over who had to walk down the stairs first. Whoever lost had to hold on to the pee-filled sheets and lead the way in the dark because we could never find the light until we made it into the laundry room.

One foot would slowly attempt to reach the first stair but wouldn't quite touch it. It would just linger, as if it were testing the water to see if it was cold. (Except in this case it was testing to see if a demon would grab it.) After a litmus test of thirty seconds passed, my trembling foot would make contact with the first step.

The haunting Stephen King sound effect that each stair made as we pressed our toes on it did nothing to calm our nerves. Also,

JoJo's nose was chronically clogged as a kid, so it sounded like the Elephant Man was gasping for air beside me as we made our way down to Satan's basement.

Once we got to the bottom, JoJo and I would glue our bodies back-to-back as we walked so we could *Cagney & Lacey* it in case demons popped out of the shadows.

I know a lot of people have a scent that reminds them of their youth. Mine is urine. To this day, that smell is reminiscent of me and the Elephant Man chasing away demons.

JoJo and I routinely made our way to the laundry room. Sometimes the washer was full of dirty clothes. JoJo and I tried not to scream as we reluctantly grabbed Mom's and Dad's unmentionables and flung them into the dryer. Then we would slump our bodies down and lean against the soothing rhythm of the washer. Sometimes we would pass out sitting up, but we were always awakened by the soft buzz of the washer as it completed its cycle.

One night JoJo had a bad case of strep throat, but it didn't stop her from crawling into my bed at night and peeing all over me. So like any good sister, I woke her sick ass up and told her she had to go to the basement with me.

She was shaking with chills and her face was dripping with beads of sweat. I remember thinking that she looked like she was going to die. Her fever had to be up to 104 or 105.

I whispered to her in a loving tone, "If you don't go with me, Satan might come up here and get you when you're all alone."

Her sick eyes cracked open and she uttered a weak "okay," as she rolled her shivering body off the bed and started to walk with me. Well, I was walking. JoJo was weaving down the hallway like a drunk driver on New Year's Eve.

As we made our way to the stairs, her body began trembling more violently. It probably didn't help that she was wearing pee-soaked PJs. I thought I would warm her up by telling her how hot Hell must be. I talked about people's skin melting off and fire roaring for all eternity.

JoJo mumbled an incoherent response. Had I been an adult, I would have realized that this was probably a sign that she was close to death. However, she still managed to walk back-to-back with me until we made it to our usual washer and dryer spot. But then all hell broke loose.

JoJo mumbled, "Do you see that?" and pointed to a corner with nothing in it.

I looked back at her face to see if she was messing with me, but she wasn't.

She held her hand out like a scary possessed child from *The Ring* as she continued pointing. She was full-on fucking seeing something in the corner.

"Is it a spider? A rat?" I was hoping she would say yes.

But she didn't. She replied, "That's *him*."

My heart fell into my uterus. She just said "*him*."

Who the fuck is *him*?

"JoJo, what are you talking about? Stop scaring me."

Then her face started shaking back and forth as if "he" were coming toward her.

I started screaming at the top of my lungs, which made JoJo scream at the top of her lungs.

"We're gonna die! Help!!!"

Above us, I heard what sounded like a herd of elephants stampeding into the basement. My mom and dad found JoJo and me on the ground holding on to each other for dear life.

We continued to scream and point toward the corner.

My parents turned their heads to see what we were pointing at, but of course they saw nothing and proceeded to yell back at me. "What?! What are you pointing at?!"

JoJo's teeth were chattering and her body was shaking, so I spoke.

"Him! Do you see him in the corner?"

My mom and dad again looked toward the corner, and my dad yelled back at me even louder, *"Jennifer, what in the hell is wrong with you?"* Jennifer was the name my parents called me when I was in major trouble (which happens often in this book).

My mother then yelled, *"What are you doing down here? It's three A.M.! And JoJo, you're sick as a dog."*

I looked at JoJo. Her eyes were pretty much rolling into the back of her head and she was shaking from her fever. I could tell she had still not regained the ability to speak, so I took the liberty of throwing her under the bus.

"JoJo crawled into my bed and then peed in it, and I didn't want her to get in trouble, so we came down here to wash the sheets, but she started speaking in tongues and I think she was seeing ghosts." There was no way I could stick up for her because I adamantly rejected the idea of being a nine-year-old in diapers.

My mom yelled, "Both of you get upstairs . . . now!"

I didn't learn the meaning of the word "karma" until I moved to Los Angeles later in life, but looking back, my karma was about to unfold for blaming this entire incident on my sister.

Later in the month, I was all alone one night because JoJo decided to do something selfish and sleep at Grandma's house. I mean pee on Grandma.

So while she was gone, I was forced to endure the demons myself.

My eyes popped open at two A.M.; I stripped my bedsheets down and stood face-to-face with the basement door. I mustered up all the strength and Jesus power within and decided that if I made the sign of the cross over and over and over while walking down the stairs, I would be protected. Kind of like the wax on/wax off move from *The Karate Kid*, but with the sign of the cross.

I opened the basement door and started my descent. My hand moved at superhuman speed. Nothing was going to harm me . . . Suddenly, and all in slow motion, my foot missed one of the stairs. I felt my body floating in the air. All nine years of my life flashed before my eyes.

I quickly thought of two things:

1. I was about to become a child of Satan!
2. Which one of my sisters would get my Cabbage Patch dolls?

Oh no, I thought. *It's happening. This is it. I asked too many questions. I'm going to Hell.*

It's amazing how time stands still before impact in situations like this. I managed to yell, but not for help. Oh no, I full-on managed to scream the Our Father prayer in its entirety.

"Our Father Who art in Heaven hallowed be Thy Name Thy kingdom come Thy will be done on Earth as it is in Heaven give us this day our daily bread and forgive us our trespasses as we forgive those who trespass against us and lead us not into temptation but deliver us from evil Amen."

And then *BOOM*.

I felt nothing. No pain. For sure I was in Hell. I knew my soul was forever in Satan's hands, so I slowly opened my eyes. Standing before me was Satan!

Kidding. I opened my eyes and nothing was there. I slowly lifted my head and then sat up.

How I wasn't hurt was a miracle.

I sat in awe, wondering if this fall symbolized my own fall from grace. Would I continue to be a devout Catholic or would I now be cursed with temptations from Satan? I knew only time would tell.

As you read on, you can make your own judgments about how hard I fell from grace.

7

Stay Home and Make It a Godbuster Night

Since we didn't have much money to ever go out as a family, I really looked forward to Sunday movies at home with everyone. The only real bummer was that we had to borrow a VCR from our neighbor. Those things were expensive pains in the ass back in the day. Not only were they a lot of money, but the damn things were really heavy. Together, JoJo and I would carry one back from the Collinses, three doors down.

By the time we shuffled back to our house, our little arms were really hurting. It was worth the free candy, though, which is why we always volunteered. Mrs. Collins would send us home with a hoard of chocolate and sugary treats. It must have been her secret sin because my parents never found out about our weekly sugar high. If only Dad's pocketbook knew where our cavities were actually coming from.

When we got back to our house, we would drop the anvil of a VCR in the living room and dash into our bedroom. We hid our collective stash under our mattress so we could later feast on chocolate in bed. We would race back downstairs with my Jesus scrapbook in hand, excited about our next religious viewing.

Sometimes my dad's friend George would join us for movie nights. Well, he would more like interrupt our movie nights, if you were to ask my mom. I think my dad must have organized it that way to get out of watching Jesus movies. George would show up with beer and snacks and plant himself on the couch to start his usual offensive commentary. Mom would eventually shoot my dad a stern look, and then Dad would haul him into the kitchen like a performer being caned off the stage. Dad didn't seem to mind this routine.

George was an atheist, but he was still welcome in our house. Mom explained that even though he annoyed her at times and had a different belief system, he was a good person with a big heart. My mom, the most religious person in our family, was accepting non-believers into our home. I liked that!

One night, we kicked off family night with *King of Kings* (1961). It was amazing that George hadn't said a word five minutes into the film. That was a record. I was actually disappointed; I enjoyed the levity he brought to our house. I noticed that he was starting to doze off, so I nudged his jiggly chest to jolt him awake. I smiled as he began watching again.

"Are you shitting me?" George came to life as he slapped his thigh and chuckled to himself. He reminded me of John Candy in *Uncle Buck*, only a bit more colorful and pear-shaped. "All seven of 'em gladiators had perfect shots? C'maaannn." He grabbed a fistful of popcorn and shoved it all into his mouth, chewing wildly as half fell out onto the floor. He grabbed a stack of our Jesus VHS tapes and started to look through them.

"*Jesus of Nazareth*. Holy shitballs, six hours? Hoo hoo hoooo," George laughed. He had eyes like Rodney Dangerfield.

Mom shot Dad her classic menacing stare to take George out of the room. Dad shot up perkily off the La-Z-Boy and summoned George to mosey on over into the kitchen. I was on to them and their master plan, and so was Mom. She rolled her eyes as she sank back into the sofa to enjoy God cinema with her four girls.

Ding-dong.

"Who is that?" said Amy.

"Mallory's coming over for the movie, remember?" my mom replied.

JoJo and I looked at each other with a finger pointing inside our throats. We couldn't stand Mallory. She was so pretentious. But Mom didn't care. She pretty much allowed anyone into her home.

"Hi, Mallory. How's your family?" my mom asked.

"They're very well. Thank you, Mrs. McCarthy," she said with a sweet smile.

"That's nice. I'll go fix you girls some snacks," my mom said as she left the room.

"You're such a brownnoser," I had to say to her.

"Takes one to know one," she replied quickly.

Mallory walked over to our pile of Jesus tapes and grabbed *Jesus of Nazareth*.

"Put this one on," Mallory said assertively as she shoved it in the VCR.

"Get real. We don't want to sit with you for six hours," said Amy.

Mallory pulled out a Bible from her overnight bag. JoJo and I face-palmed ourselves when we realized she was sleeping over.

"Oh no, my mom's babysitting you?" I said.

"My parents are gone for the night. Now shut up so I can read my Bible." She rolled her eyes and fingered through her Bible, flipping pages but not reading anything.

"You don't even care about God, you just pretend to!" JoJo said with an accusatory finger pointing at her.

"God hates you and He loves me! You're just jealous," she said.

"You don't even go to church! Wait, I take that back, you're a Chreaster!" I bounced back like a crazed girl on *Jerry Springer*. ("Chreaster" is the term Catholics made up to call other Catholics who go to church only on Christmas and Easter.)

"That's because we're so holy we don't need to go to Mass every Sunday like you sinners," she snarked back.

"You are so jealous of my relationship with Jesus!" I said defensively.

"God, you guys are dumb," Lynette said, rolling her eyes.

"You guys are just bitter because you're so poor and your house is disgusting," Mallory said, flipping her hair.

I wanted to punch her in her face, but Mom came back in with snacks to feed the bitch.

It was a defining moment for me to realize that people could fake being religious. How could an atheist like George be a kinder, more respectful person than our "Catholic" neighbor?

It became obvious to me that even the holiest of households could have family members who were faux Bible-thumpers. Even at this young age, I thought that being a good person was the most important thing. It was all about motive. I wanted to find my happy place in the world. And I had a lot of motivation to drive me there.

8

Jesus's Baby Mama

I was twelve. Sister Betty says, "So, children, today we are talking about how Mother Mary got pregnant without having sex."
My mouth hit the floor so hard I was sure I broke it. I raised my hand.

"What now, Jenny?"

"What are you talking about? How can someone get pregnant without having sex?"

"Mary was born without sin. That's what the Immaculate Conception means. Mary was told by angels that she was going to be carrying God's son. Then she became pregnant."

"That doesn't make any sense. She had to have sex with someone," I shouted.

"It's a miracle," she replied.

"So can this miracle happen to me? Can I get accidentally pregnant right now?"

"No."

"Why not?"

"Because you were born with sin."

"Why was I born with sin?"

"Because Eve was tempted by Satan and then made Adam take a bite of an apple so we now have sin."

"Wait a minute. You are saying that we are all born sinners because Adam and Eve were hungry and ate an apple?"

"Well, they were supposed to be strong and not be tempted, but they chose to disobey God and became sinners."

"That stinks. Why aren't we angrier at Adam and Eve?"

"Well, Jenny, Adam and Eve is more of a myth . . ."

"What?!"

"We don't really know who the first human being was. We use that story as an example of how and why we are born with sin."

"Whoa whoa whoa," I replied. "Again with the fake story. So I think what you are trying to say is that the Bible is a fictional book."

"No, that's not what I'm saying. There are many true stories that Jesus's disciples wrote down and put in the New Testament."

I replied, "Yes, but last week you said most of those stories were not written down until one hundred years later. How can they even get anything right?"

"You have to have faith, Jenny."

"I'm starting to think that word means trust someone else's beliefs."

"Do you believe in God, Jenny?" she asked.

"Well, duh, yeah."

"How do you know He exists?"

"Because you told me I had to believe it," I said with the utmost honesty.

"But we have never shown you proof that He exists, so what makes you continue to believe that we are right?"

"Well, you scared me into thinking I will burn in a pit of flames for all eternity, so I'm pretty sure I'll just believe in God in the off chance you are right."

"But don't you feel God's love in your heart?" she asked.

I took a moment to reflect to see if I could feel God's love in my heart and I could.

To this day, I don't know if that was the love I had for myself or if God was doing a happy dance on my heart, but it felt good.

I smiled and looked back at Sister Betty. "Yes, I do feel God's love in my heart."

"Then have faith that we are right."

I nodded to her once again, having faith she was right.

"Okay, now, class, I want you to take out a piece of paper and draw a biblical scene that we will hang in the hallway for parents' day. Please draw something that you have learned in class over the last semester."

A week later, my mom came home from parents' day. She was holding the picture that I drew in class that day.

"Jenny, what the hell is this?" She held up the picture of the biblical scene I drew.

"It's the Virgin Mary, pregnant."

"But look what you have Joseph saying to Mary."

The bubble above Joseph's head said, "Are you sure this baby isn't mine?"

9

Like a Virgin

I was in seventh grade when Madonna's "Like a Virgin" came out. I remember staring at the TV with my mouth hanging open, watching her frolic around in a sexy wedding dress and rocking crucifixes like they were trendy accessories. I truly believed that the lyrics, "touched for the very first time," were written for me. How was this creature named Madonna able to talk about sex like that and still call herself Madonna? How come she was allowed to roll around on the ground humping the floor and wear see-through shirts? I wanted to be her.

But my mother came into the room and stopped in her tracks when she caught a glimpse of Madonna "for the very first time." "There's that sinner!" she said.

"Madonna?" I replied.

"Yes, who would ever wear a rosary as a necklace?"

"Um . . . nuns do," I said as quietly as possible.

My mother did not enjoy my quick point of view on the matter. "That's different," she said.

"How so?" I asked.

"Because Madonna is using them to be sexy. Nuns wear them

because they are respecting God. Madonna is evil. There is no way any mother would name her child Madonna and let her look like that. She's trying to lure men into her sexually spun web of promiscuity."

Wow, that's awesome, I thought.

My mother pointed to the TV just as Madonna began practically masturbating on a boat in the canals of Venice.

"I like her music," I said casually. "I think she's pretty."

"Jenny, you can't look up to girls like that. She's a disgrace to God. What self-respecting man wears a lion head? That's obviously symbolism for bestiality and that is a serious sin. You wouldn't be friends with someone who slaps God in the face, now would you?"

"No, of course not," I said.

My mom patted me on the back and walked out of the room.

I ran to my bedroom and pulled one of my two thousand rosaries off one of my two hundred crucifixes and put it around my neck with a scapular for good measure. I then proceeded to pull one shoulder of my sweater down to reveal my training bra strap. I walked in front of the mirror and began flipping my hair as I danced around and sang every lyric. "Like a vir-r-r-r-gin, touched for the very first time."

It felt so good to be doing something I wasn't supposed to do. It kind of felt like when I would wake up in the middle of the night to steal a bunch of JoJo's trick-or-treat candy (which I did only two times, JoJo . . . okay, maybe three). I couldn't understand why being naughty felt so good. So I went to the free therapist—our priest.

"Forgive me, Father, for I have sinned."

"What is it?"

"Well, I kinda just want to know why it feels so good to sin."

"Hmm . . . Let's start with which sin you are referring to."

"Well, I'm not even sure if this is an actual sin, but I know it's not right."

"Go ahead, continue."

"I like Madonna," I whispered.

"Well, I love Madonna," Father Colin replied.

"You do?!" I replied with glee in my voice.

"Yes, I do," he said.

"Oh my God, that's freaking awesome! I thought you were all, like, uncool and just played chess all day long and watched *Leave It to Beaver*."

He laughed. "Why would you think loving Madonna would be a sin?"

"Well, she wears a rosary as a necklace."

"What's wrong with that?"

"That's what I said! Oh my God, you are the coolest priest ever! My mom also said that Madonna was the spawn of Satan."

"What?! Why would she ever say something like that?" he asked.

"I don't know. My mom also said that Madonna is definitely not a virgin like she claims to be."

"What? What has gotten into your mother? Of course Madonna is a virgin!"

"Wow, you really are a fan of Madonna. Maybe you can convince my mom to let me go see her in concert."

Silence was all I heard for about twenty seconds. I could see his shadow remain motionless through the confessional screen that separated us. "I think we are confused. I'm talking about the Virgin Mary, our Madonna," he said.

"Oh . . . hmm. Awkward. Well, what do you think of the MTV Madonna?" I asked.

"I don't know who you are talking about. There is only one Madonna, the Virgin Mary," he responded firmly.

I left confession that day with the realization that I had to come up with my own interpretation of why it felt good to sin. The only I thing I came up with was that it was like chocolate. Even though everyone says it's bad for you, we all enjoy it. You just have to balance it with eating right or choosing your sins wisely, like selecting a quality chocolate. The same goes for sinning. Not too much, but just enough makes life way more satisfying.

Fast forward to eight years later. I am twenty and have experienced heavenly bouts of freedom. When I heard about the upcoming release of the Madonna *Erotica* CD, I nearly lost my shit. She was more risqué than ever. I was craving a Jesus-like fix. They almost went hand in hand now. Madonna and Jesus. One and the same. Tearing off the cellophane from my *Erotica* CD felt like unwrapping a present on Christmas morning. I slid the CD into my stereo and my heart sang while my body started thrashing around provocatively to the beat. I was experiencing an all-time high of the chocolate factor. Just then my mom charged into my room like a bull in a china shop. She was behaving like a tyrant, and I'd never seen her quite like this before. It scared the shit out of me so much that I fell off my bed.

"I know that voice! Get her out of this house now," Mom demanded.

I wanted to scream something stupid like, "I'm twenty, Mom!" or "Leave Madonna alone!" but I knew it was hopeless.

Momma preached and she made up her mind. She slammed the CD on a retaining wall outside. There was fire in her eyes as she muttered about "the sinner wearing a cone-shaped bra symbolic of two cornucopias" putting a curse on our home. As if destroying my *Erotica* CD weren't enough, she went on a tangent bitching about how her suspicions of bestiality were confirmed. She grabbed the album, whose back cover had an image of Madonna sucking on an elephant's trunk, and tossed it into the fire. I watched it melt down and turn to ash.

That night, Mom went through all my shit to make sure I got rid of every trace of Madonna memorabilia. Touched for the very last time.

me with some serious Aqua Net hair

10

If Gluttony Is Evil, Why Are So Many Catholics Alcoholics?

My family was getting ready to go to a ceremony at our parish, where they were going to announce the winner of the Traveling Mother Mary.

In case you aren't that Catholic and don't know what that means, it's basically a four-foot statue of the Virgin Mary that travels around the world. It is then up to a lucky parish to choose an even luckier family that is holy enough to have it in their home.

At thirteen, the problem I was having at the time was that puberty and religion just didn't mix. I was embarrassed by the whole thing and prayed we didn't win. If we did, my mother would be required to put Mary on a table in our front living-room window to display to the whole neighborhood, much like in the movie *A Christmas Story* when the father of the Ovaltine kid wins the leg lamp with fishnet on it and his wife is horrified that he is displaying it for all to see.

To make matters worse, the other obligation is to have an open-door policy for strangers to come in and join the rosary reciting all day and into the night. That would be beyond embarrassing.

When we arrived at the church, my mom and my baby sister Amy, who was my mother's minion, were ecstatic. Me and my two other sisters, Lynette and JoJo, were not that happy. My older sister, Lynette, at this point was goth and had half of her head shaved bald and the other half dyed jet-black. She looked like she was going to sacrifice a chicken, but she never did. Probably because she turned out to be a vegetarian. JoJo just did and felt whatever I did and felt, so she seemed equally embarrassed.

Once we got to the parish, families ran up to greet us, telling us that the McCarthys were one of two finalists.

"God damn it," I accidentally said.

My mother snapped her head around and gave me her famous evil eye, then continued to talk to her fans. "So who is the other finalist?" she asked.

"It's the Baruchs."

If this were a movie, it would be directed by Quentin Tarantino. The camera would zoom into my mother's face, with an eyebrow raised, and then scan the room for her archenemy.

Now I wanted to win. I wanted to win and shove our trophy . . . uh . . . our victory up Diana Baruch's ass. Screw being embarrassed. I wanted to win!

Father Patrick took the stage and began the presentation talking about the significance of the Traveling Mother Mary statue—about how it had graced many homes around the world.

"But now Mary has made it to Chicago to be displayed at one family's home for one year. This family was chosen after much consideration as the holiest family in the neighborhood."

The McCarthys and the Baruchs joined Father Patrick and

stood on each side of him while my mom and Janet Baruch exchanged competitive grins.

Father Patrick continued: "The holiest family on the South Side of Chicago, who has never missed Mass and who best displays purity of truth, love, and devotion, is . . ."

My mom's eyes grew large, but mine grew smaller as I scratched my itchy nose with my middle finger, catching Diana Baruch's stare.

With a perfect *American Idol* dramatic pause, Father Patrick continued. ". . . the McCarthys!"

We all jumped into the air and screamed as if we had just won $2 billion. The parish applauded us. As I turned around to look at the Baruchs, they had already gotten off the stage and disappeared. Part of me felt bad. Even though I hated them, I couldn't help feeling sorry for people when they were sad.

When the parish officials delivered Mary to our home, I couldn't have been more embarrassed.

As a teenager in a poor family, I was already incredibly ashamed about my house. Now throw a four-foot Mother Mary statue into the mix and, well, it's darn right humiliating. What made up for it, though, was how proud my mother was.

She put Mary on a table surrounded by flowers she handpicked. She felt so proud, and she loved opening her door to strangers to come inside and kneel in our living room to pray all day and night.

Living in a house with strangers praying the rosary out loud for a year is really not normal, though.

I tried to get used to it, but there were so many old people that our house started to resemble the set of *Cocoon*.

Right around this time, I met a boy who I really, really liked, but I knew I could never let him know where I lived. A Virgin Mary statue is not an aphrodisiac. He went to a public school.

In the past, I would be terrified to talk to any kid who didn't attend a religion class, but when I hit thirteen, I wanted to make out with all of them.

"Hey, Derek."

"Hey, Jenny. Can I come sit in your basement and hang out with you?"

"Um, no," I said. "Why don't I just come over to your house and we can make out?"

"That's dope," he responded, using the perfect 1986 slang term for "yes."

I went over to his house.

I hardly got past the door before he jumped on top of me. He did something I hadn't experienced yet at the age of thirteen—he kissed my neck.

It felt naughty. He seemed to either be really enjoying my neck or just not confident yet about his ability to French kiss. It's kind of like when a guy tells you he doesn't like going down on girls, but it's really because he has no idea what the hell he's doing.

Anyway, after about an hour of necking, I was getting bored, so I pushed him off me.

Derek began laughing at me.

"Why are you laughing?" I said.

"Don't know," he responded.

"You're weird," I said.

"Later," he quipped.

And with that, we broke up. I wish it were that easy to break up in my thirties.

I went home and saw more old people filing into the house. I didn't want to deal with it anymore. I wanted Mary to go away—now. I walked inside and was pulled by an old lady to sit next to her and pray.

She handed me a rosary and I began to recite a Hail Mary.

I spotted JoJo doing what I had taught her to do, which was to sell rosaries to old ladies as "blessed rosaries" and we would split the money seventy-thirty, because it was my idea (even though I had JoJo do all the work). This was an early sign of the incredibly sinful entrepreneurial skills you will continue to read about throughout this book.

"Psst, JoJo." I waved my hand for her to come over and save me.

As she walked closer to me, her eyes widened. She quickly sat down next to me and whispered, "What's wrong with your neck?"

"Nothing," I said. "Why are you looking at me like that?"

She then grabbed my arm and pulled me into the bathroom.

I took one look and screamed at the top of my lungs. *"Aah-hhh!!!!"*

That asshole Derek had given me hickeys. Not just a couple of hickeys. He gave me thirteen huge, bloodsucking hickeys.

"Why would you let someone do that to you?" JoJo asked. "You look so stupid."

I defensively cried back, "I didn't know what he was doing! I thought he was just really into my neck. I didn't know! What am I going to do?"

"Well, now I think is the perfect opportunity to ask for a raise," JoJo said. "I want fifty-fifty for the rosary money."

"JoJo, stop that. I'm in a crisis right now!"

"I'm in a crisis now too! Christine Szarski is about to get her eleventh Cabbage Patch doll! I can't let that happen! I need to go buy three of them right now!"

If it were anything other than a Cabbage Patch doll, I would have fought her, but I was sympathetic to JoJo's problem. I caved and gave her the fifty-fifty split, even though I knew she would never tell my mom about the hickeys anyway.

The next day at school, word got out that I had thirteen hickeys on my neck. I was terrified of only one person in school finding out. That's right—Diana Fucking Baruch, who was one grade older than I was.

"Jenny, Diana just found out about your hickeys," said Ann Krybus.

I ran to the school bathroom and threw up. I was so scared. We were supposed to be the holiest family in the neighborhood, with the Virgin Mary as our prize.

I had no doubt that if my mom found out about this, she would either return the Mary statue or make me live at the altar reciting Hail Marys until I died.

I got home from school and ran upstairs to put on the thickest sweatshirt I owned, which happened to have Mickey Mouse on it. It was 96 degrees outside with 100 percent humidity. I didn't care. Cover Girl makeup did nothing to cover my hickeys. My Mickey Mouse sweatshirt was the only solution that worked.

I went downstairs, sat in the kitchen, and tried to act nonchalant as sweat dripped off my nose.

My mom walked in and said, "Jenny, it's ninety-eight degrees outside with one hundred percent humidity."

"No, Ma, it's ninety-six degrees."

"Get out of that sweatshirt. You must be dying."

"No, I'm fine."

JoJo was sitting at the table with me and saw that I had started to panic. "Ma, it's the new thing in school. Big sweatshirts, even when it's hot outside."

"Oh, really?" my mom responded. "Well then, where's yours?"

JoJo quickly answered, "Oh, I couldn't find mine."

"It's in the closet, inside the box labeled winter clothes," my mom said.

"Oh, thanks. I'll go put it on."

Moments later, JoJo returned to the kitchen wearing a large, thick sweatshirt. Beads of sweat started pouring down her face too. She leaned into me and whispered, "Now I want sixty-forty."

"No way," I whispered back. "How about I buy you a Michael Jordan poster?"

"Deal."

I knew I had JoJo's lips locked, but my instincts were telling me that Diana Baruch had yet to play her hand.

Ring, ring.

"Hello," my mom answered the phone.

My eyes watched every social cue on her face for a change in behavior.

A second later, I didn't need to watch her face. It all came out in her voice. "What are you talking about? Jenny doesn't have thirteen hickeys on her neck."

My whole body started trembling. This was it. My life was about to end.

"Who is this?" my mother yelled.

I wanted to run away, but I had made a total of only two hundred dollars in the rosary business and now I had to give JoJo half of it. My mom slammed the phone down and walked over to me.

I had a sweat mustache and my armpits were squirting water like hoses.

"That was a priest who suggested that I not allow you to go to school tomorrow with hickeys."

"That's crazy. There are no priests at our school."

"That's exactly what I was thinking. It must be some prank caller." And she walked out of the kitchen.

JoJo and I sat there stunned and soaked, like we were swimming with our clothes on.

"I hope you learned a lesson in all of this," JoJo said to me.

"Yes. I did. Only get hickeys in the wintertime."

11

Monkey See, Monkey Do

There was a new priest in town. A hot one. His name was Father . . . well . . . let me think of a good alias. His name was Father Andrew.

Imagine one sexy beast of a hot priest turning up on the block of *Desperate Housewives* and rattling the minds and bodies of all those sexually deprived women. Well, my neighborhood turned into that. You could see the abstinence in the eyes of every housewife and the amount of days since they were last humped practically written on their foreheads: 17, 65 . . . 481.

Father Andrew was about thirty-five and resembled a younger Tom Selleck—mustache and all. He was in amazing shape and had the same spunk and charisma as Zack Morris. He was like one of those characters you see in movies: the hot young teacher who bonds with all the schoolkids and plays dodgeball with them in the parking lot.

All the students thought Father Andrew was cool.

But to all the moms, he was prime meat to salivate over.

It was survival of the most predatory animal in the wild. Women and closeted men alike would go to great lengths vying for

Father Andrew's attention. One mom dropped off a homemade lemon meringue pie she made especially for him and she literally fainted as she walked to the back of his house, exposing a secret corset that cinched her waist and squeezed her torpedo tits together and pushed them up to her chin.

I was only in seventh grade when Father Andrew came into our lives.

I didn't really understand sexual fantasies yet, so my daydreams of him would be me falling and him picking me up in his arms and carrying me all the way home. I can only imagine what all the moms' fantasies were, but who wants to think about that? Gross.

Anyway, Father Andrew's popularity became obvious when his 9:45 A.M. Sunday Mass would sell out like a Justin Bieber concert. The women would even clap and dab the sweat off their bodies after his homily. I remember looking around at all their faces thinking, *Really?* Women were in a trance, swaying back and forth with their blouses unbuttoned in the hopes of Father Andrew sneaking a peek at their new brassiere.

It was an outrageous spectacle.

When Father Andrew would clock in for confessions, I would always get so pissed off because the line was so long. I was a regular customer, so all these newbies were totally ruining my quick stop just to come and flirt with the priest. They treated confession like an audition for an episode of *Red Shoe Diaries*. With confession, you had a choice of doing it face-to-face or going behind the screen so the priest couldn't identify you. Needless to say, every mother in line chose the face-to-face seat.

I can only imagine how many of them were complaining about

how awful their husbands were as they pulled Kleenex from their heaving bosoms to wipe the crocodile tears of loneliness from their lying bedroom eyes and Bambi lashes coated with waterproof mascara. What a scene it was.

A few months into Father Andrew's debut, a wickedly entertaining competition started to unfold. Which family would Father Andrew choose to become close friends with? The rectory in the church soon became filled with Bundt cakes, oatmeal cookies, rum cakes, and a multitude of other confectionary fancies to tempt him into people's homes.

But Father Andrew was no dummy. He was Irish. He went where the booze was running thick—my house. The McCarthy house was filled with laughter and the smell of scotch.

I remember thinking, *Wow, this is really fun.* I also remember being a bit confused by the fact that gluttony was considered a sin, yet alcohol and desserts were given to win someone's affection. It was just one of the many contradictions in my childhood.

Once word spread that the McCarthys were in the lead, the Baruchs decided to throw a welcome party for Father Andrew. Yes, the fucking Baruchs. I even caught word that they hired a Christian rock wedding DJ. When someone hires a DJ to a party on the South Side of Chicago, it's like the Holy Grail. It doesn't get more classy than that.

The neighborhood was all up in arms as to who would be invited. Clearly not us. So, being the clever and competitive woman that my mom is, she decided to throw a party on the same night. Now it was up to Father Andrew to choose where he wanted to go. Being the dignified diplomat that he was, he promised both families that he would make an appearance since we lived only a couple of houses away from each other.

Oh no, I thought. *Game on.*

Remember the movie *Annie* when Annie and the other orphans scrubbed every inch of the orphanage while singing "It's the Hard-Knock Life"? Well, that was my sisters and me. We scrubbed and scrubbed the house in preparation for this party. My dad even erected a new bush outside our home that had been recently destroyed by a drunken uncle who fell into it.

The McCarthys were going all out.

As the day grew closer, Father Andrew came over to talk to my mom.

He tried to encourage her to bury the hatchet by extending an olive branch to Mrs. Baruch. I remember peeking around the corner to eavesdrop and covering my mouth to keep from laughing out loud. There was no way in hell my mom was going to give in to that wench of a woman.

With clenched teeth and a fake smile, she said, "Father Andrew, I would really enjoy that and would love to have her join us at my home to have one celebration instead of two."

I heard that Mrs. Baruch was given the same speech by Father Andrew. But, as expected, the parties stubbornly remained on the same night in separate houses. When I woke up for school the day of the party, there was a buzz in the air.

Parties were given only for graduations, but seeing that this was a special occasion to keep up with the Joneses, everyone was invited.

During school, I ran into Diana Baruch in the hallway. She had her usual "don't fuck with me" look on her face. She snarled and said, "Just so you know, I invited the entire class to my house tonight, so don't be expecting anyone at yours." Then she flipped her hair in my face as she walked away.

Could she be right? Would everyone go to her house instead of mine? This would be a huge blow to my social status as a seventh grader. It was scheming time. Think, Jenny, think. Then it hit me.

I ran through the hallways looking everywhere to find Blaire Starecki. She was more Polish than a Polish sausage and I knew her grandma had a stash of Polish liquor in the attic. I never drank liquor—well, except for church wine—but I knew a lot of my friends were already experimenting with drinking.

I quickly found Blaire and talked her into going to her grandma's house after school in hopes of scoring a bottle of the Polish stuff. Blaire liked the idea, so I quickly spread the rumor to my friends that I would get them some alcohol if they came to my house for the party. Needless to say, everyone RSVP'd quickly.

After school, Blaire and I successfully pulled two bottles of liquor from Blaire's grandma's house. I had never heard of this kind of alcohol. It had a homemade label on the front of it with a handwritten word: MOONSHINE.

I ignorantly asked, "Is moonshine some type of vodka?"

Blaire replied with an equal amount of naïveté, "Hell if I know."

Then we made our way to 7-Eleven, stole ten Big Gulp cups, and took them back to my place.

I had never seen my house so clean. You could have performed brain surgery in the living room. My mom had her best church outfit on while preparing her famous cocktail meatballs. I could tell she was nervous and excited about hosting this very special event in the neighborhood. It was like Vanity Fair's Oscar party vs. the Acme party. My mom wanted ours to be the Vanity Fair party, of course. It had to be.

The Baruchs' party was first up that night. All the neighbors could be heard dancing and singing with the DJ. Even though we had two hours before our party was scheduled to start, my friends who had RSVP'd for alcohol were already at my house.

My mom was freaking out that her Vanity Fair party was looking more like a Nickelodeon party, so she shooed us all to the basement, which was fine with me because I had some bartending to do. Once down there, I passed out the Big Gulp cups to my friends and filled them all up to the rim with this moonshine stuff. I also topped off my own cup and proceeded to drink. The next thing I remember, I was standing in our now-crowded living room with my friends and neighbors, violently puking everywhere. And by everywhere, I mean everywhere. Furniture, walls, people—even Father Andrew. I remember people screaming because all of my friends started riding the puke train, and soon enough the entire room was Jackson Pollock'd in vomit. It looked like a scene from *The Exorcist.*

Then I faintly recall waking up from being dragged away by my hair. I'm pretty sure it was by my dad. I also remember puking all over him and the bathroom for what seemed like two days. I definitely remember my mom giving me a bath and not enjoying the realization of that.

That night, I cried myself to sleep like a baby.

To say my mom was mad at me was the understatement of the

year. She was humiliated and furious. I completely ruined her night to shine.

I tried my best to throw everyone else under the bus to lighten the punishment, but it didn't work.

Once I recovered from liver failure, my mom made me go apologize to Father Andrew and confess my sin.

As I sat with him experiencing my first and worst hangover ever, he wanted to know why I would think that getting liquor would make my friends like me.

I replied sincerely, "Well, that's why you became friends with our family in the first place. I saw my parents buy you liquor and it worked. So I thought it would work for me."

The sheepish look on Father Andrew's face made me realize how dumb he felt. Children do learn from watching adults, and no doubt he was guilty himself.

We sat in silence for a minute, and then he said, "Looks like I need to be doing a penance rosary with you." He knelt down next to me and recited the rosary with me.

I had so much respect for the fact that Father Andrew saw his own sins in my actions.

I wished all adults were like Father Andrew.

12

GOD: Thou Shalt Not Have Strange Gods Before Me.

JENNY: I'm Cool with That But... Who Are You?

I was thirteen.

"What now, Jenny?" asked Sister Harris.

"I'm confused."

"What else is new? What are you confused about now?"

"I'm confused about the First Commandment: 'I am the Lord thy God. Thou shalt not have strange gods before Me.' I don't understand exactly what that means."

"It means we should worship only God, no one else," Sister Harris explained.

"Okay, define 'worship.'"

"To praise and adore. You shouldn't put a picture of an elephant on the wall and praise it as God."

"What if God is an elephant?"

"God is not an elephant," said Sister Harris.

"How do you know God is not an elephant?"

"Because I know."

"But how?"

"Enough."

These were the back-and-forth conversations I had with nuns

at the school that my dad worked his balls off to afford. I quickly came to realize that nuns weren't mentally equipped for my investigations, so my questions were not well received.

I was truly stumped by the First Commandment. I was stumped by this rule as to who God is. If the Catholic Church doesn't know what God is, how can they tell me not to worship other gods? What if I accidentally bought the wrong snow globe with the wrong god inside it?

I raised my hand again with more question marks floating in my head. "Sister?"

"What?"

"Jesus always referred to God as a 'He,' so that's why the Church believes it's some sort of a male species, right?"

"Yes, Jenny."

"Well, we refer to a boat as a 'she.' So maybe Jesus was calling God a 'He' like a gendered pronoun."

"What is wrong with you?" said Sister Harris. "Why do you ask these questions?"

"Um, because we're in religion class right now."

"Why do you question your faith?"

"Because I'm trying to understand it."

"But that's where faith comes in," Sister Harris said. "Trust that the things you don't understand were already understood for you and have faith we are right."

"Really? So believe everything you say and don't question it?"

"Just have faith."

I left school that day totally committed to God as a dude with a beard and a staff. I was going to have faith! I wasn't a trouble-maker. I was a truth seeker.

I was tired of the nuns dismissing me as if my inquisitive nature just brought piss and vinegar to their classrooms. The truth was that I just wanted to be more self-aware of my religion so I could continue being a good person and avoid accumulating unnecessary sins. It was in their best interest if they wanted me to remain holy as a subservient Catholic girl!

Now I'm fourteen years old.

I'm in my new high school. It's the first day of school at Mother McAuley, a prestigious all-girls school taught by nuns, of course. I loved that school. I'm proud to have gone, but I suffered some major hard times there.

Many of the girls came from affluent families, but my family made the sacrifice to spend all of their hard-earned money on our education. When the other girls found out my family was struggling financially, they used it as a tool to belittle and torment me. It took me a long time to find my core group of trustworthy girlfriends.

The first girl I became friends with was Christine Higley. She had a dollface and the hottest older brother, Alexander. Christine was timid, a real quiet one. I quickly learned why. Her family was not only extremely religious; they were ridiculously overprotective. I thought my parents had me on a tight leash. Christine was on house arrest. Her mom used angel cookie cutters to shape sandwiches and included handwritten bizarre "godspirational" quotes in her lunch every day.

I remember sitting at the Higleys' dinner table and observing how disconnected their family was. Christine would try to have an open dialogue with her mom to talk about things that were more interesting to her than God, but she was quickly dismissed and ignored. Coloring outside of the biblical lines was strictly forbidden.

After several teenage years of isolation and resentment, Christine ended up moving to Las Vegas and becoming a showgirl. But the back pages of a Nevada newspaper clearly illustrated that that wasn't enough excitement for her since she went a step further and became a full-on dominatrix. Her brother was destined to be gay, and he finally came out of the closet a year later. It was their parents' worst nightmares come true.

The point is, Christine was a cry for help and Alexander was way too hot to be straight.

It was around that time that I came to understand that it was possible to tip your God scale. Everyone needs balance. What was enough to make God proud? What was too much to live by? I had so many questions.

I constantly looked for guidance and still remember the conversation I had with my new teacher, Sister Nancy, in high school.

"Girls, we will now refer to God as the Creator, not as the Father," said Sister Nancy.

I nearly lost my uterus when I heard this.

"Yes, Jenny?"

"What do you mean you changed it to Creator instead of Father? I thought God was a He?"

"No, we believe God is not a sex. God is a Creator of all. God is."

"Since when?"

"Since now," Sister Nancy replied.

"Says who?"

"Says us."

"Who's us?"

"Different sectors of Catholicism."

"Different what? This is ridiculous."

"What is ridiculous?"

"How you guys change everything, your rules."

"Things change," said Sister Nancy.

"Yes, I understand that. But when you teach us to follow the Ten Commandments and then switch the meaning behind them, how do we know what to believe?"

"What do you mean we switch the meaning?"

"In grammar school, I was taught the meaning of the First Commandment: 'Thou shalt not have strange gods before Me.' When I inquired as to who that God is, so I don't accidentally worship a strange one, my teacher said, 'It's Jesus's dad, a guy.' Now God doesn't have a gender?"

"God is not defined by a gender," said Sister Nancy.

"Okay, so five years ago if some dude believed what you believe now, a no-gender God, and brought this concept to the Catholic Church saying, 'Stop worshipping that guy with a beard and a staff and worship the correct God,' and showed everyone a picture of a light ball, the Church would have said, 'Stop worshipping that strange god! You are breaking a commandment!' Right?"

Sister Nancy just stared at me, not knowing how to answer the question.

So I continued. "So this dude and whoever else believed in a no-gender God five years ago are now burning in a pit of flames for all eternity. They will suffer because they were ahead of their time."

"You are exaggerating the situation," said Sister Nancy. "If someone was Catholic and believed in God and led a good life, they will not burn in Hell for all eternity."

"But if you break a commandment and die with a sin on your soul, you are damned to Hell, right?"

"Yes."

"Okay, so this dude appeared to have a strange god. He didn't match the Church's concept and dies without knowing to confess it, so he's currently with Satan."

"Go to the principal's office!"

"Huh?"

"Go. Leave."

And that was my first day of high school.

me at middle school graduation

✛

13

Jesus Was My Justin Bieber

I was always fascinated by all things Jesus.

My mom was a pope fanatic, but I was very much obsessed with my man J.C. This was no secret as it was celebrated in my house daily.

The commemorative I ♥ NY T-shirts that became popular in the 1970s gave me the idea to design my own I ♥ J.C. shirt. I wore it so much it was practically fused to me like body paint. I rocked that thing like it had to be everybody's business. That is until Greg Baruch took a match flame to it. Not even my waterworks could save my precious J.C. memorabilia. Ashes to ashes. Dust to dust. Greg broke into maniacal laughter as my bedazzled Jesus top burned to the ground.

Losing the top wasn't going to ruin me, though. I had memories of Jesus everywhere. Most of my friends had posters of Michael Jackson on their bedroom walls. Not me. Oh no. My rock star was Jesus. I had framed pictures of my love cut from the latest tracts from the Jehovah's Witnesses Watchtower Society that I religiously stole from a neighbor's front porch. If the Avon catalog had a picture of a Jesus pillow for sale, it was getting cut out and added to my shrine. My side of the wall looked like a curbside memorial to worship Jesus, with dried flowers and rosaries held on by Scotch tape bordering the photographs.

Even though I was embarrassed about religious stuff during puberty, Jesus was the exception.

Meanwhile, my sisters would plaster pictures from *Teen Beat* magazine all over their sides of the walls to exalt their flavor-of-the-month crush. Scott Baio lasted a whole season, but I was sure that my Jesus crush would last a lifetime. I was in deep. I even had a Jesus scrapbook, for Christ's sake. I was snipping out text to complement my shrine like a serial killer writing a ransom note.

Sex was never discussed in my house, so we girls were left to deal with puberty on our own. So right around the time my boobies started growing, I noticed that Jesus was hot!

I would stare at his poster and want to brush my fingers through his perfectly blow-dried hippie hair. Those baby blue eyes would look right through me. I dreamed that Jesus was performing live in concert. I was the crazy teenager sobbing in the front row, hoping he would sweat on me while playing his guitar.

Based on the Bible, Jesus was not only a great guy, but he listened and cared. Chicks dig that. I wish there was a part in the Bible talking about Jesus's bitches following him around because I would have totally been one of those bitches back in the day. But the Bible talked only about men who followed him everywhere. Hmm . . .

Anyway, I mentioned my love of Jesus to a few of my friends and they called me a disgusting pervert. Well then, whoever was in charge of painting his picture should have made him ugly as sin, because if you're going to put a hot picture of God's son everywhere, it's kind of hard to go through puberty and not think he's sexy.

One time in high school, I snuck my boyfriend over to make out and dry hump in my bedroom. I closed my door and threw my cheerleading pompoms on the floor as he slowly lowered me onto my waterbed.

Yes, I said waterbed.

My boyfriend's young, stubbly face rubbed against mine as I felt his hard-on through his tight jeans. It felt so incredibly naughty. He pulled my shirt up and started playing with my nipples over my bra. It was sending lightning bolts through my body that were so intense I couldn't help but moan. With every dry hump, he would press his hard-on against the crotch of my jeans and rub faster and faster. My breathing got louder. I rubbed my fingers across his back and felt his muscles working so hard to maintain the intense rhythm. My eyes started rolling into the back of my head because my body was experiencing such pleasure. I started squirming my body around uncontrollably. Then he leaned into my ear and whispered, "You are so beautiful. You drive me crazy, Jenny."

I felt a rush between my legs that made me know I was about to have an orgasm. Just as I was about to surrender myself to this intense pleasure, my eyes spotted Jesus staring at me. Those soft, beautiful blue eyes I had always gazed at in my dreams now looked angry at me, like a jealous boyfriend.

Oh my God, I thought. *Jesus is totally watching me right now.*

The climb of my orgasm had all but disappeared as my boyfriend continued to dry hump me. I didn't know what to do. I now felt dirty and shameful. I couldn't continue with Jesus staring me down the way he was.

I had to do something.

"Can we stop for just a second?"

The look on my boyfriend's face was like he had just been violently awakened from an amazing dream. "What's wrong?" he said with concern.

"I'm sorry. I can't do this while Jesus is watching."

My boyfriend was silent for a second, and I could see his puberty brain trying to defend what we were doing in the hopes of continuing our amazing dry-hump session. "How do you know Jesus is watching?" he asked.

"Because I can see him right behind you."

"Jesus is behind me right now?" he asked.

"Yes, and he doesn't look very happy."

My boyfriend slowly began to peel his body off mine and stand up. He pressed his obvious boner into his body as much as possible and then slowly turned around.

His eyes were lined up with Jesus. They both just looked at each other, like a staring contest in a Western showdown. Then he finally spoke.

"You're right. He does look pissed off right now. What do we do?"

My eyes quickly scanned the room. I spotted a magazine with Cyndi Lauper on the cover. I quickly ripped off the face, grabbed tape, and stuck Cyndi on top of Jesus's head.

My boyfriend and I looked at each other to see how we felt. We nodded our mutual approval and then threw our bodies onto the waterbed.

As the dry humping continued, I looked at the poster and felt good having Cyndi Lauper watch me dry hump instead of Jesus. For security reasons, I thought it might be a good idea to move our risqué activity to under the blanket in the off chance Cyndi's head fell off the wall.

Once the blanket covered us, my boyfriend started to unzip my jeans. His hand slowly reached between my legs as he slid his finger inside me. I was so incredibly aroused. I was so grateful that finger blasting didn't count as premarital sex. I felt my body about to reach orgasm again.

Then I heard: "Jennifer! What the hell is going on?"

I whipped the blankets off and standing in the doorway was my mom. I died in that moment. A part of me is still there in that waterbed, dead.

My boyfriend was frozen with his hand in my pants and I quickly bolted up. My mom started screaming and my boyfriend ran out. My fear tuned out most of what she was yelling, but I remember key words like "disappointed" and "ashamed," along with questions like "What kind of a girl did I raise?" Then she looked over at my Jesus poster. "What the hell happened to Jesus?"

"I didn't want him to see what I was doing."

My mom ripped Cyndi Lauper's face off Jesus and yelled, "If Jesus has to cover his eyes, then you shouldn't be doing whatever it is that you're doing!"

She stormed out of the room and I fell back onto my waterbed, crying.

When I lifted my head up to take a breath, I noticed my Jesus poster.

When my mom had torn Cyndi Lauper off his face, she had pulled Jesus's eyes off with it. Thanks for solving that problem, Mom.

14

GOD: Thou Shalt Not Covet Thy Neighbor's Goods.

JENNY: But What If My Neighbor's Shit Is Really, Really Awesome?

From an early age, my parents attempted to teach us how to appreciate the things we have and to not envy our friends' stuff. Unfortunately, watching them envy their friends' stuff made it extremely difficult for us not to do the same thing.

My dad grew up in a small house with twelve brothers and sisters. He slept in a closet because his house had only two bedrooms. When Vietnam came calling for him at the age of eighteen, it was like an upgrade. He would have his own bed for once.

Unfortunately, and as expected, the stories of him walking the front line in Vietnam were nothing short of horrific. It took years to get some of these stories out of him, but eventually the vault began cracking and stories started spilling.

There were so many people dying around him, he expected not to survive. Just on the off chance he did, he sent his military checks home to Chicago so his mom could put them in his bank account and he could build a life for himself once he was out of the war.

After two long years of serving on the front line, Dad got to come home. He was never injured during the war, but on the plane ride home he was bitten by a mosquito and caught malaria. As if the emotional scars from Vietnam weren't painful enough.

Once back in Chicago, he was determined to start a life for himself. With the money he saved over two years, he was going to put a down payment on a home and hopefully meet the right gal and start a family. This was his lifelong dream.

Sadly, what took place next was the finishing touch to destroying my dad's dream of creating a good life. His brother forged his name and spent all of his Vietnam money. It was gone.

Needless to say, my pop was devastated. This wasn't the type of devastation that caused him to get mad, punch his brother in the face, and move on. This was the type of devastation that dug deep into the core of his soul and remains to this day.

My perception was that my father dealt with this by coming to terms with the fact that money is always supposed to be a struggle to get. To him, it always seemed that as soon as he got some money, it immediately went away. He didn't know what else to do to earn a good living, so he decided to go to beauty school because that's where the hot chicks were and where he could have as much sex as possible. Smart guy. He obviously had a great time because he married the hottest beautician in the joint—my mom.

My mother came from a poor household too, so they both had a lot of experience with putting food on the table with no money in the bank. My dad took a job at a steel plant and my mom got her license as a beautician. She worked from home and did the majority of hairstyling for our neighbors. Her strategy was awesome when we were desperate to get dinner.

Mom would wait for a neighbor to walk by our house and say, "Hey, Mike, your hair is looking a little long. You want me to trim it?"

Everyone would say, "Yeah, it is pretty long. Okay."

And then she would collect five bucks from them.

That night, boom bam, we were eating noodles with ground chuck for dinner.

When people say to me, "Jenny, you really are a scrapper in Hollywood," I know that this is why. I learned it from the best.

I'll always find one way or another to feed Evan.

No one really had money in our neighborhood, but there was always one family that seemed to have the best toys, clothes, and lawn décor: the Baruchs.

Those damn Baruchs would rub it in our faces too. My Big Wheel had a crack in the seat, so when I rode it, you could hear me coming from a mile away because my ass was scraping the concrete. I really wanted the new Big Wheel that had pink pompoms.

Soon after mine broke, Diana came whizzing past the front of my house with the fucking Big Wheel with pink pompoms.

"Hi, Jenny. Do you like my Big Wheel? You will never ride it. Ever!"

Whenever I would say to my mom, "Why do the Baruchs get everything? It's not fair!" my mom would reply, "Jenny, don't be jealous and envy what other people have. It's a sin."

The next day I would catch my mom out on the porch squinting her eyes to watch Mr. and Mrs. Baruch put up the most amazing Christmas decorations on the South Side of Chicago. I could hear my mother say, "Look at that. That is not fair. They shouldn't be allowed to have those beautiful decorations. They are sinners. We deserve them. We've never missed a single Mass. Ever!"

I so badly wanted to tell her, "Didn't you just say we shouldn't envy other people's stuff?" but I couldn't. My mom worked so hard to take care of us that I could never be mad at her for all of her contradictions no matter how wishy-washy they were.

This is where I created a belief system to help me cope—that rich people were evil.

I think this was the only way to not be depressed about not having money.

There is even a religious song that proved the theory: "Blessed are those who are poor . . . for someday you should laugh."

I knew I couldn't help my parents at this young age to get money, but I knew I could make them laugh. I would regularly put on shows to give them a chuckle to help ease the pain of poverty. I was hoping this would hold them over until I was old enough to help them financially.

Our monetary strain got progressively worse through the years. In my teenage years, it was even more difficult not to have the material things I wanted. I so desperately wanted the new sparkly blue Schwinn ten-speed. I had a picture of it up in my room and would pray for it to any saint who would listen.

One afternoon, I was sitting on my porch when Diana Baruch rode past my house on the blue Schwinn bike that I had been praying to God for. She paused in front of me and said, "Like my new bike?" and then rode off laughing.

I couldn't believe this was happening again! How could I not envy?

I mean, come on, God!

Then a miracle happened. Well, actually two miracles. The first was that my mom took us to McDonald's.

McDonald's for us was like going to Disneyland. It was considered a luxury. One reason we were able to go was that my mom scored two perms from nuns at the convent and made a whopping fifteen dollars! The other reason was that McDonald's was promoting that Monopoly game where you collect stickers for each square and win big cash. My mom was collecting them from everybody she knew. Even the nuns would give them to my mom when they saw her.

So off we went to McDonald's and came home to devour the food.

My mom pulled the Monopoly squares out of the bag and uncrinkled the paper Monopoly game board she had been gluing the other squares on.

Just as I was sinking my teeth into a hamburger, my mom started screaming, "Oh my God! We won! We won!"

She jumped up and down as if she had won a car on *The Price Is Right*. I ran over to look at her Monopoly board game and all the stickers were covering every square.

I too began jumping up and down and screaming.

My mom then ran outside and started screaming, "We won twenty-five thousand dollars!"

Friendly neighbors hurried over to celebrate and jump up and down with us. I was so excited. God heard my prayers.

Of course, I immediately thought of myself and asked, "Can you buy me that ten-speed I want?"

My mom, still jumping up and down, suddenly morphed into a philanthropist with the power of Oprah. "You all get one!" She pointed to all of us kids with her mouth open and her eyes wide and bright.

"Woohoo!"

Now I was jumping up and down as if I had won the Showcase Showdown on *The Price Is Right*.

My mom ran back inside the house to call my dad at work. I followed her in to maybe catch a scream from my dad on the other end of the phone. Mom asked Dad's boss to page him and have him call back immediately.

While we waited for my dad to call, my mom shouted out all the bills she would pay off with this money. I was a teenager, so all I cared about was making sure I got my damn dream bike.

I asked my mom to guarantee that I would get my blue Schwinn. She was so elated with joy she just kept screaming, "Yes! Yes! Yes!"

With that confirmation, I went over to the Baruchs with a pep in my step. I was cocky with a new attitude. I envisioned myself riding past their house showing off my ride.

I stopped in front of their house and shouted to Diana's bedroom window, "Hey, Diana! Diana!"

Moments later she came to the front door. "What?" she said in her usual bitch tone.

"We won twenty-five thousand dollars and my mom is buying me the same ten-speed you have, and I thought you should know so you don't confuse yours with mine when it's parked in front of my house."

"You're a dork," she replied. She slammed the door and went back to her room.

She was right. I was a dork, but I was a winning dork! I ran home and continued to celebrate with my family. My mom told me that she talked to my dad and he was leaving work early to take our prize into McDonald's to cash in.

That was a huge deal.

Dad never missed work. He couldn't afford to.

Mom told me that our win was announced at my dad's work and the steel plant celebrated for him. It was a good day for the Mc-Carthys. A really good day.

When my pops pulled up to the house, we all greeted him by jumping up and down on him. He giggled with a delight I hardly ever saw from him.

My parents sat down at the kitchen table and went over the game together.

My dad smiled. "Wow, we really won. This is really gonna help. Let's go take a ride to McDonald's and talk to the manager."

Holy shit, I thought, *we get to go to McDonald's twice in one day! Woohoo!* We all jumped in the car to go claim our prize and have dinner as a family at my new favorite restaurant in the world.

As my dad started the car it misfired, which would normally cause him some audible grief and cussing, but this time it was symbolic of our newfound life, as if the car were saying, "Giddyup." My entire family had a healthy glow as if we had just come back from vacation. Nothing could bring us down. Mom looked at me when Michael Jackson's "Ben" came on the radio. I was smiling and singing along. Not even the sounds of Satan could faze me and kill the high my family was on.

When we got to McDonald's, my dad told us all to order whatever we wanted while he talked to the manager. My dad explained to the manager that we won the Monopoly game and needed to know what the next step of the process was. The manager congratulated us all and looked at the Monopoly game to confirm our win. His smile slowly faded as I heard his lips slowly mouthed the words "Youuuuu didn't wiiiiiiiinnnnnnn. You used the same piece twice."

I quickly looked at my parents, who looked down and realized their mistake. The defeat and sorrow that came over them caused a little piece of me to die in that moment. It was the longest, most awkward, painful moment, as my mom and dad and their four daughters stood there with long faces, staring at the McDonald's manager in complete shock. Again, being a teenager, I thought of myself first. My bike. My dream bike! I had already told Diana I was getting one. The whole neighborhood thought we won. Everyone at my dad's work thought we won.

All I could feel was shame, embarrassment, and anger. The manager could see the look of devastation on each of our faces and gave us our dinner for free. We all shuffled over to a booth and ate in silence.

Swallowing that food was like swallowing glass. We were all sucking back tears from the rise and fall of our McMoney as we suffered through our last McMeal. I remember looking at the life-size Ronald McDonald statue and wanting to punch him and bleach the stupid red smile off his face. Once I got past my own depression about the bike, I could see the true devastation in my parents.

I so badly wanted them to get ahead financially and felt hopeless at age fifteen. Looking back now, I can see how this didn't help my dad's belief system of having money one minute and then it disappearing before his very eyes the next.

This was the day I made a promise to myself.

I was gonna make it up to my parents.

The McCarthys would overcome this.

Someday, I would pay off their bills and make them proud. But first, I had a lot more sinning to do.

Dad and the girls

✝

15

The Purpose of Lent?
I Give Up

Every year, Christians prepare for the risen Jesus during the season of Lent. Well, not exactly.

Every year, Christians celebrate the anniversary of people preparing for the risen Jesus during the season of Lent. Well, not exactly.

You see, nobody prepared for Jesus to rise from the dead because nobody knew ahead of time that he was going to rise from the dead. So for the six weeks before Easter, nobody was wearing sackcloths and ashes, nobody was fasting or abstaining from meat, and nobody was giving up things they liked. But today, we prepare for the risen Jesus—even though his resurrection was about two thousand years ago. Which is like saying that someone is preparing for a wedding anniversary. Hey, you prepare for the wedding, not the anniversary!

This is why so many people have a hard time dealing with Lent. We're asked to suffer to make ourselves more presentable for Jesus. It's like losing a bunch of weight so you'll look like a dreamboat in front of your onetime sweetheart at the high-school reunion. But when your former sweetheart sees you, he doesn't realize you had to drop twenty pounds to look so hot. On the other hand, Jesus knows what you looked like before and after. And supposedly he loves you either way. So what's the point?

Lent is a lot like the story of Cinderella. You start out with ashes on your forehead and end up wearing a beautiful dress.

In between, it's a time to atone for your sins with heaps and heaps of sacrifice.

And let's face it, the Catholic Church likes the idea of sacrifice a lot.

> BOY GEORGE: Do you really want to hurt me?
> Do you really want to make me cry?
> CATHOLIC CHURCH: Uh, yeah.

Holy people say that sacrifice wards off the devil. Then they turn right around and mention the Bible passage in which Jesus fasted for forty days and forty nights in the desert. As I recall, the only visitor Jesus had during that time was . . . the devil.

The folks who invented Lent—no, it wasn't Jesus's idea—decided that just like Christ's time in the desert, it should last forty days. Actually, from Ash Wednesday to Holy Saturday it's forty-six days, so it looks like the first thing someone ever gave up for Lent was math.

For those forty or so days, you're supposed to give up something you enjoy—or something you're not supposed to enjoy but you do anyway.

When I was young, one of the first things I tried to give up for Lent was lying. I quickly found out that wasn't a good thing to do, or maybe I should say that wasn't a good thing to stop doing because someone soon will ask what you're giving up for Lent.

If you tell the truth and say, "I'm giving up lying," they will say, "You've been lying? About what?"

And if you lie about giving up lying, well, that's that.

When I got older, I tried to give up alcohol.

I was okay for a while, but then I really started to miss it. I imagined I was living in the time of Christ and I had been invited to a wedding at Cana. All of a sudden, Jesus comes up to me.

JESUS: I just changed a bunch of water into wine. Have a glass.

ME: Uh . . . geez, Jesus . . . this is kind of awkward. I gave up alcohol for Lent.

JESUS: Really? How did you find out what I was planning to do for Easter?

ME: Long story. Anyway, thanks but no thanks.

JESUS: Are you sure? Everybody's saying my wine tastes a whole lot better than the wine they ran out of.

ME: Jesus, are you tempting me?

JESUS: Geez, this is kind of awkward.

If you think that's crazy, imagine the hallucination I had when I broke my Lenten resolution and started drinking again. And it's not enough to give up chocolate or lying or alcohol or gossip. You also have to give up meat on Ash Wednesday and all Fridays during Lent.

Why Fridays? Maybe it's because Jesus died on a Friday.

Or maybe it's because Long John Silver's has a surplus of fish that it has to get rid of by the weekend and it worked out a deal with the Vatican.

By the way, this rule of no meat on Fridays was for Americans only. So truth be told, I wonder which bishop owned stock on the East Coast fish harbors, considering this rule only came into practice in the 1960s. Sounds fishy to me.

Anyway, if you're a meat lover like I am, giving up meat for even one day is a real sacrifice. No hamburgers. No meat loaf. No steak.

But if you're a vegan, giving up meat is no sacrifice at all. This doesn't seem fair.

Shouldn't the Catholic Church say, "No meat on Fridays and no vegetables or salad on Wednesdays"? Let's balance out all this sacrifice.

So for all of these reasons, Lent remains a mystery to me.

The Catholic Church says sacrificing to cleanse your soul of sin is something you should like. Therefore, for Lent you should give up something that you like. Okay then. The next time Lent rolls around, I'm giving up sacrificing.

16

Girls Gone Wild

College. Holy shit.

I attended Southern Illinois University. It was voted the number one party school by *Playboy* magazine, so I was all over attending that campus. Also, it was really easy to get into. My parents didn't want me to go there, but I was denied entry from all the other universities, so they didn't exactly have a choice.

After attending Catholic school for twelve years, the thought of being unsupervised elated me. I couldn't wait to hit the bars with my big hair and fake ID.

My dad took the six-hour drive with me from Chicago. I was waiting for the "don't get pregnant and don't do drugs" talk, but it never came. It felt good that Dad trusted me enough to at least use a condom and not overdose.

We pulled up in front of my dorm, and I will always remember the feeling that I had vividly. It was the feeling of freedom. I unpacked my dad's car and brought everything up to my room in one hour. Then I politely hugged my dad and shoved him out the door.

I heard silence. No parents, no sisters, no nuns, no one telling me what to do. I quickly pulled out the pack of cigarettes I had been hiding for four years and sucked one down. With every puff, I danced around my room. I couldn't wait for a dorm neighbor to offer me a beer.

That night, I went out to nickel draft night and met Laura. She was a junior, but she must have recognized the look of "I'm ready to party" on my face and quickly made friends with me. Laura and I then proceeded to go out every week, getting drunk, making out with boys, and begging restaurants for free food. Soon we gathered a regular crew of girls and proceeded further to intoxicate our bodies and wreak as much havoc on campus as possible. My friends' favorite thing to do was to dine and ditch. The problem, besides running out on the bill, was that my crew enjoyed having me be the last one to leave the restaurant. They would take turns peeing and then would knock on the glass outside the restaurant staring at me, leaving me alone to ditch the table myself.

As I successfully ran for my life every time we dined and ditched, I was hit with huge amounts of guilt. I would run and cry without letting my friends see. I wasn't afraid of breaking a commandment so much as I was saddened by the waitress who was counting on the tip to feed her family. I felt bad about it, but peer pressure always won.

Speaking of peer pressure, drugs quickly became popular among my friends too. Fortunately, the drugs back in my heyday were pot and mushrooms. There wasn't really any coke, heroin, crystal meth, etc., on our campus. Just good old-fashioned hallucinogenics. Looking back on this time now, I'm grateful for the drugs that were en vogue because I hadn't yet built up enough self-esteem to stand up to peer pressure at that time and those harder drugs really ruin people's lives. So I turned into a stoner and mushroom expert. I had posters of the Grateful Dead; I knew every word to Pink Floyd's *The Wall*. And I started to grow dreadlocks. I became so good at shrooming that I started offering tours on the weekend to help people through their trips.

As odd as this may seem, I was really good at it. I realized during this time that I was really connected to other people's energies. I was able to figure them out and calm them. I was like the mom people went to when they were tripping their balls off. This is not something you want to find as your calling, but later on I would come to realize how valuable it was in being able to identify negativity and illusions that people were using to get to me.

My first year in college, I did very well academically. By the second year, I was running out of money and could barely pay my bills, which made my grades suffer because I was busy working odd jobs instead of studying. One of the jobs was cleaning fraternity house bathrooms. I knew I could get hired for that because I spent the majority of my time bent over scrubbing. I wish I could have called home to ask for money, but I knew my parents didn't have any, so I quickly learned how to expand my scrapper career.

I would ask boys if I could come over to their place and make out. Then I would go over and raid their fridge for frozen pizzas and canned food and take off. Once most of the boys were on to me, I resorted to bouncing checks for food. I was bartending at the time, but all that money went toward my rent and I had no way of surviving without sinning.

Then I came up with the really good idea of creating a VIP parking pass that allowed you to park anywhere on campus. I made these and then sold them to freshmen for fifty bucks. It was lucrative, but it really started to wear on my soul.

I thought that if I was sinning to get by, I should at least save the money to use for good, like tuition and books. I promised myself and God that I would not use my money to party or buy clothes. Then my crew of friends came to me with the biggest temptation of all.

"Jenny, we are all going to Daytona Beach, Florida, for spring break. Want to go?"

Damn it!

I looked at my giant vodka bottle filled with fifty-dollar bills. I was in agony. This wasn't fair.

I envisioned them all coming back with tans and STDs, and I couldn't bear to miss out on the action. But I did what any smart Catholic girl would do and said no. My friends understood, which pissed me off more. They all packed up their suitcases and wedged eight girls into a '78 Chevy Nova. I watched them pull away, limbs sticking out of the car and horn honking.

I hated being poor. I thought back to that passage in a church song: "Blessed are those who are poor . . . for someday you shall laugh."

I wasn't laughing.

I was depressed and angry.

The next day, the campus was empty.

There was no one around. Every living soul from SIU went on spring break, and the only good thing about it was that I could park anywhere I wanted to on campus. I went to grab a slice of pizza from Pag's Pizza (had to mention it for all those SIU alums). While I was in there, two guys walked in and ordered slices and I overheard them talking about heading to Florida for spring break.

Just as I was about to close my ears so I didn't have to suffer anymore, I heard one guy say, "Too bad we didn't post a sign for help with gas. We still have room in the car."

Before I could even think about it, I shouted, "I'll go!"

With that, I was sitting in the back of a beat-up, disgusting van that didn't have backseats. I was on the metal floor next to a drum kit and what I thought for sure was a body bag. I think I was in shock as I sat there finally realizing I was with two strangers. I started praying to God for a lifeline.

"Please, God, don't let me get raped or killed. I don't know what I was thinking. If you can get me back home alive, I promise to never steal food or sell illegal parking tickets again."

Then I started smelling pot.

Even though I was a stoner, I never risked it while driving. My fellow road trippers passed the bong back to me and I politely refused. My body started shivering because the van didn't have heat and I was sitting on metal with holes in it and I could see the road as we drove.

"Um . . . how long until we get there?" I asked.

"We're driving straight through, so we should be there in twenty-five hours."

I would have started crying, but my tears would have froze. I don't know how many hours had passed when the car pulled into a stop. I asked where we were and the weirdos replied, "Chattanooga."

I closed my eyes and tried to flash back to fifth grade when we learned the map and attempted to count how many states we had left until Florida, but I was interrupted with . . .

"Hey, how much money you got on you?"

Shit.

I'm fucking dead.

This is it.

They are going to rape me, kill me, and then rob me.

I replied like a Canadian. "What do you mean, eh?" I asked with a chuckle.

"We could use more."

"How much more?"

"Like another twenty bucks."

"Okay. Just let me pee and I'll come back and give it to you."

I ran to the truck stop bathroom, which smelled worse than anything I had ever smelled before. I went over my options and it was clear I didn't have any. Cell phones hadn't been invented yet, and I was in a truck stop in Tennessee. I've done some pretty stupid things in my life, but this was the worst by far.

I came back to the van and handed the guys a twenty. They grabbed it and handed me a hot dog.

"It was buy one, get one free," they said.

I was starving, so I devoured it, as they did theirs.

Soon we were back on the road.

I could feel us getting farther south because my body stopped shivering from hypothermia. My thoughts remained on how dumb I was and how much fun my friends were probably having. Finally, we crossed the border into Florida, which the men celebrated with about ten bong hits each. They said we were about an hour away. I had never been so grateful about anything in my life.

"Where do you want to be dropped off?" one dude asked.

"Whitehall Hotel," I said.

"Whitehall Hotel? There is no Whitehall Hotel," he said during a bong exhale.

"Yes. My friends are staying there. It's on the beach," I said sternly.

Both the guys looked at each other and scratched their heads. "We'll ask when we get into town."

"Great idea."

After about an hour we pulled into a gas station.

The guys opened up the back door of the van and the Florida sun nearly scorched my eyeballs. I had been sitting on the floor of a van with no windows the whole trip. I was literally blinded by the light.

I semi-crawled out of the van and stood up on the ground. The breeze took my breath way, it was so warm and tropical. If that wind could have talked it would have reassured me, saying, "Everything is going to be okay."

A gas station attendant approached the car and my stoner dudes asked where Whitehall Hotel was.

The gasman replied, "There is no Whitehall Hotel."

I immediately yelled, "Yes, there is! My friends are there. I know that's where they are staying. I helped them make the reservation. Whitehall Hotel, Daytona Beach."

The stoner dudes giggled. "Well, there's your problem. We're in Panama City."

"Okay, so how much longer till we get to Daytona?"

"We're not going to Daytona. This is our stop."

"What the fuck are you talking about?"

"We said we were driving to Florida. You assumed Daytona. We were headed to Panama City."

"You're kidding."

"Nope. Not kidding."

"Well, can I hop on a bus to get there?"

They laughed and replied, "We are on the gulf. Daytona is on the Pacific side. You're kind of fucked, but you can come to our girlfriends' house and see if you can hitch a ride with somebody there."

Daytona was *the* place to go for Spring Break in the early '90s, so I had hoped that the stoner dudes were right about possibly hitching a ride with someone. I headed over to the house of the chicks who were boning these stoners to figure out what to do next.

As I sat down on a beanbag filled with cat hair, I saw two girls in the other room giving me dirty looks. I heard the stoner dudes trying to tell them to be cool to me. I had really long bleached-blond hair that was down to my butt and I wore tight jeans. It was not a look you can easily gain new girlfriends with.

I sat on the beanbag for four hours with no one coming to talk to me or offer help. Once in a while I would see a girl peek around the corner to see if I was still there. I was. I started crying a little and decided that my only option was to leave and try to find a ride elsewhere.

I snuck out the front door and walked down a neighborhood street in Panama City.

I finally reached a 7-Eleven and tried to call my friends in the hotel to get help. I used four dollars in quarters trying to reach them. No answer.

Why would they answer? I knew they were all drunk on the beach.

I was really scared at this point. The only thing I felt I could do was pray. I asked my guardian angels for help.

"Dear guardian angels, please protect me and guide me to someone who is safe and can help me."

I hung out at 7-Eleven for about two hours until I decided to walk to the beach. There were a lot of spring breakers partying, so I thought I might as well pretend to be one of them.

I was quickly drawn into a few party circles with men who all looked like steroid monsters. I was given a beer . . . and another . . . and another.

The next thing I remember, I was being dragged to a stage for a wet T-shirt contest, kicking and screaming like I was about to be hanged. I cried and begged the guys to put me down to no avail.

I was plopped onto a stage with ten sluts who were gyrating in G-strings. I crawled to the nearest exit of the stage, but it was blocked. Then hoses were pointed at us and we were soaked.

I kept thinking that this all had to be a nightmare.

First of all, I don't know anyone. Second of all, I'm in a wet T-shirt contest with no tits (pre-boob-job years).

I stood there in shock, watching the girls practically have sex with themselves onstage while thousands of men videotaped them. Then they all started yelling at me for not moving around like a ho.

I tried fleeing again, but I was blocked by a beefcake.

I was left with only two choices: get naughty or punch the beef-cake blocking the exit in the face. Just as I was about to throw a right hook, I heard an announcement that the winner of the contest would win five hundred dollars in cash.

Damn it! Here comes more temptation.

If I won, I could catch a flight to Daytona Beach.

Was this my guardian angels' way of saying, "Here's some help"?

My hips began shaking left and right. The men burst into cheers. Then I turned around and shimmied my butt the best I could. More cheers from the crowd. It was kind of liberating until I looked to my left and saw the ho next to me tear her shirt off and bounce her wet, naked boobies all over the stage. It was absolute mayhem. It was as if the animals were unleashed, and the roar of the crowd was deafening.

I ran toward the exit and kicked the beefcake in the face as hard as I could.

I grabbed my bag and took off running down the beach in my wet T-shirt.

As I ran, I was applauded by more spring breakers.

I just wanted this all to end.

When I finally felt I had escaped, I plopped down on the sand, laid flat on my back, stared at the sky, and asked my guardian angels for other help besides a wet T-shirt contest. I closed my eyes and passed out.

When I opened them again, it was sunset. I sat up and felt crispy. I had never been to Florida before and I had no idea how intense the sun was there.

I got up and walked to find a bathroom.

Even the warm Florida breeze now hurt my face. I realized that I had been out in the sun all day with no sunscreen, and since I'm Irish, I usually burn in forty-five minutes of Chicago sun. I couldn't imagine what all-day Florida sun could do. I made my way to a diner and went into the bathroom.

My face was not only red but forming blisters all over.

It looked like someone had thrown a grease pan on my face.

I started crying as I bounced my finger on all the blisters. I looked like a monster.

I ran to another pay phone and begged God for one of my friends to be in the room. If it was sunset, it meant they were probably back in the room getting skanked up to hit the town.

Ring, ring.

"Hello?"

"Oh my God, oh my God. Who is this?" I asked.

"It's Erin. Who the hell is this?"

"It's Jenny. I need help. I'm seriously fucked."

I went through the whole story. All I could hear was uncontrollable laughter, but my friends immediately got me a plane ticket and flew me to Daytona Beach.

Sadly, when I arrived, they had to take me to the emergency clinic because I had suffered such severe burns on my face. I was ordered to stay in my room for the remainder of spring break. I had to watch my friends come in and out of the room and have sex with strangers as I laid there staring at the ceiling with bandages on my face.

As days passed, I reflected on how wise my intuition really was and how I should have trusted it to not go down to Florida in the first place. I wondered how many more times I would have to go through crazy shit like this until I finally learned my lesson.

Well, it turned out to be a shitload more times, but at least I can say that I won the next wet T-shirt contest. *Whoop whoop. Jiggle jiggle.*

me with only slightly less serious hair

17

O Holy Night

My heart was racing. I kept looking behind me to see if I had ditched the cops. Just to be sure, I continued to floor the gas pedal.

Thoughts of "How the hell did I get here?" raced through my head. I looked down at my car seat and saw the illegal parking passes I had made in college along with the checkbook I used to bounce checks for food.

"Oh yeah, that's probably how."

I weaved in and out of traffic and witnessed countless senior citizens flipping me the bird. Who knew they had such pizzazz?

I pulled off an exit and hid out in a parking lot next to miles and miles of cornfields. The song "Total Eclipse of the Heart" was on the radio. I remember it like it was yesterday because I burst into tears while singing the words "Once upon a time I was falling in love, but now I'm only falling apart." I was a hot mess. This is not how I had planned to leave college.

How would I explain this to my mother?

. . .

Ding-dong. My heart was racing as I waited for my mom to open the front door. "Jenny, what are you doing home?" she asked.

"At least I'm not pregnant!" I shouted.

"What in God's name are you talking about?"

I moved past her, walked into the living room, and plopped down on my childhood sofa.

"I went broke. I couldn't afford to pay rent and eat. And when you don't have those things, it's time to go home. I dropped out. Well, it was more like I got chased out of college."

My mom burst into tears. "I'm so sorry we couldn't send you any more money. We are struggling to get by. We have zero in our bank account right now."

I looked around our disheveled home. I was hoping so badly I could take care of my parents someday, and now I felt like a failure in every way.

Even the Baruchs had moved on up and out of our neighborhood.

I hugged my mom and promised I was going to figure out a way to help her and my dad. Someday I was going to pay off every one of their bills.

She kissed me on the cheek and then asked, "Is all your stuff in the car? Let's get you unpacked."

"Um, I left everything behind. I was in a hurry."

Actually, I really didn't have anything to take. I was borrowing all of my roommate's clothes. The only thing that I left there were my tampons, and they were stolen from a restaurant.

I opened the door to my old bedroom and took a huge leap into the air to plop onto my waterbed. I couldn't wait for my body to jiggle on it. I hit the bed hard.

"Ouch!" That wasn't what I was expecting. My mother had put a box spring mattress in place of my waterbed mattress to make it appear there was still a bed there.

Who does that?

My sisters JoJo and Amy, who were still living in the house, ran into my room, excited I was home. JoJo squeaked with joy: "Can I have your fake ID?" Followed by Amy: "Can you teach me how to smoke a joint?"

Spoken like true Catholic schoolgirls.

I responded, "No and no. I need my fake ID, and Amy, I'm pretty sure I smoked myself sober. I don't want anything to do with it."

"I can't believe you're moving back in. Don't you feel like a loser?"

"Yes, thank you. You guys are so awesome. You always know what to say to make me feel better. How's Dad doing?"

"He's working three jobs. Tuition at McAuley is killing him," said JoJo.

My heart sank.

"I feel so bad. He works hard for all of us to get great educations and you two are asking for my fake ID and wanting to learn how to smoke pot while I just ran from the cops. He would be so proud."

I plopped back on my bed, forgetting it was a box spring. "Ouch! Damn it! I've got to figure out a way to get us all out of here. I can't live like this anymore."

"Well, hurry up and think quick. Christmas is a few weeks away and none of us got anything for Mom and Dad."

"Let me think, let me think . . . Hmm . . . Got it!"

D*ing-dong*. An old lady opened her front door and smiled. JoJo, Amy, and I began singing, "We wish you a merry Christmas, we wish you a merry Christmas, we wish you a merry Christmas and a happy new year."

I then held out my hand. The old lady smiled with delight and shouted, "Christmas carolers! Let me get you some money."

My sisters and I high-fived each other as the old lady came back with her purse. She dug inside for a good minute and handed me a quarter. "Merry Christmas, girls!" she exclaimed, and then shut the door.

"It's going to take us forever to make money," Amy said.

"Well then, let's start moving," I said.

Ding-dong.

"Rudolph the red-nosed reindeer had a very shiny nose. And if you ever saw it, you would even say it glows. All of the other reindeer used to laugh and call him names. They never let poor Rudolph join in any reindeer games. Then one foggy Christmas Eve, Santa came to say, 'Rudolph, with your nose so bright, won't you guide my sleigh tonight?'"

"Oh, girls, thank you for that song. You are such sweet carolers. Merry Christmas!" And she closed the door.

"She totally stiffed us!" said JoJo.

Ding-dong.

"You know Dancer and Prancer . . . um . . ."

Amy tried to cover the confusion. "Donner and Blitzen, Comet and Cupid and . . . um . . ."

SLAM.

"Shit," I whispered.

We hit about thirty more homes and counted five bucks. Amy and JoJo were losing steam and bitching like brats.

"I can't do this anymore," Amy said.

JoJo joined in. "My toes are frozen. It's like thirty below outside."

"Don't be stupid," I said. "It's, like, five degrees outside."

I went to the next house and walked up the stairs. My shivering finger hit the doorbell and a man answered.

"O holy night . . ."

I was waiting for my sisters to chime in with me, but I heard nothing. I turned around and saw that they had completely ditched me. I turned back around, realizing I was doing a solo performance.

". . . the stars are brightly shining . . ."

SLAM.

"Damn it!" I whispered. I couldn't believe my sisters ditched me.

My voice is pretty awful by myself, but I was determined to make quick tax-free cash without doing anything illegal anymore. So off I went to the next house.

Ding-dong.

"Joy to the world, the Lord is come! Let Earth receive her King . . ."

"Darling, how old are you?" asked this adorably sweet lady. I was afraid to answer her, because how many twenty-year-olds hustle the neighborhood singing songs for cash by themselves?

I was sure as shit the answer was none.

"Um, I'm twenty," I said in the softest voice possible.

"It's thirty below zero outside. Why don't you get a job indoors?" she asked.

"I need to make some quick cash to buy my parents Christmas presents," I said with the utmost honesty. "I don't really have time to job hunt, fill out applications, et cetera."

"That is so sweet of you, dear. So this isn't for a boyfriend?"

I laughed. "The only man worth me freezing my butt off for is my dad. I love him. He's the hardest-working guy I know."

"Hold on a sec." She left and came back with a twenty. "Hope you get them something wonderful!"

"Oh my God. Thank you so much. You have no idea how grateful I am! Do you want me to sing you another song?"

"No!" She giggled.

I laughed, thanked her again, and followed it with a "Merry Christmas!" I Christmas caroled by myself every day for eight days. I made $250. I had at least fifty doors slammed in my face, one person threatened to call the police, and one offered me an extra ten bucks if I sang and shook my ass back and forth. Of course I obliged.

On Christmas night, we all sat around the tree, and I felt so good handing my parents a gift I know they deserved.

My mom opened the envelope and read it out loud. " 'The last time you both went alone somewhere was your honeymoon. Here is one night free at the Love Shack Inn to get your freak on, but don't make any more babies. We can't afford them. Merry Christmas. I love you. Jenny.'"

"Wow, Jenny, that is so thoughtful. How did you pay for this?" my mom asked.

Amy said, "The idiot Christmas caroled for eight days."

My mom and dad started laughing. Then my mom said to me, "Jenny, you have always amazed me with your clever ways to make money. You kill me." They both got up and hugged me.

They had no idea just how clever I was about to get.

Pickles

18

Can Someone
Kill Our Dog, Please?

Our family dog was named Pickles. She was a mutt with scraggly black hair. If Pickles were a person, she would totally be Janeane Garofalo.

Living in a house with four little girls, Pickles had to endure getting dressed up in gowns and wigs for years. We loved her and treated her like a fifth sister.

When I was about ten years old, I was getting ready for school one morning when I noticed Pickles pushing like she was trying to poop. I stood there in shock because Pickles never pooped in the house.

"Mom, Mom, something is wrong with Pickles. It looks like she is trying to poop, but nothing is coming out."

My mom ran over and started yelling for my dad. "Dan, come here. I think something is wrong with Pickles."

My dad and all my sisters joined in to watch Pickles bear down.

Suddenly a black blob came out of her and hit the floor. The blob had legs! Pickles was giving birth! I was amazed and disgusted at the same time.

We all stood there not really knowing what to do. Within fifteen minutes, there were three blobs on the floor that came to life. Pickles continued to bear down and push, and we were all waiting for the fourth blob, but it never came.

After giving birth, Pickles started looking weak, and my mom and dad took her to the hospital. She had a dead, deformed puppy inside her that she couldn't deliver. They removed the pup and brought Pickles back home to care for her litter.

It's a beautiful thing to watch animals care for their pups. Without words, their energy and attention radiate love.

In the months that followed, we watched people come over and adopt all of Pickles's babies. I wondered how Pickles didn't get upset that people were stealing her babies. Another amazing thing about animals, I guess.

Our family had no idea how old Pickles actually was because my dad had found her on the side of the road with rubber bands around her snout and rescued her. But while I was in high school, Pickles started to slow down. She wouldn't chase down birds anymore, her hair started to get wiry, and, by my senior year, she started to stink.

My whole family ignored the fact that Pickles was getting older. There was no way we would ever think about putting her down. But after a couple more years, Pickles had tumors all over her body. When I pet her, my hand would go up and down because of all the bumps. It was obvious she had cancer and there was nothing we could do about it. Pickles started to live behind our couch. She wouldn't move from there. All we would see was her little tail sticking out. Then she no longer had the ability to control her bowels.

People would come over, sit down in our living room, and say,

"You know it reeks of pee in here." We all kind of knew it but ignored it because solving the problem would mean putting down our beloved dog. And that wasn't going to happen.

When I came back from college, I was amazed to find Pickles still alive. Well, she wasn't really alive. She couldn't walk, she was loaded with even more tumors, and she would pee and poo on herself.

I sat down next to her and petted her while singing the song I used to sing to her when I was little. My heart was breaking. I was mature enough now to see that Pickles was in pain and that we were all being really selfish.

I confronted my mom. "Mom, I think it's time."

"Time for what?"

"To put Pickles down."

"Oh, Jenny, I don't want to talk about that."

"She's in a lot of pain. I don't want her to die either, but she can't live like a blob on the floor and suffer. We have to let her go." I could tell I was getting through to my mom.

Her eyes started to tear up and she said to me, "Okay then, you take her in."

"What? Why me?"

"Because you think it's time."

"I can't do it. I love that dog."

"Well, no one will do it, Jenny, so either you take her or she stays."

I felt sick to my stomach, but I wanted to help Pickles get out of pain and agreed to be the brave one in the family. "Fine. I'll do it tomorrow. Let's make sure everyone says their good-byes."

The next day my entire family surrounded Pickles. We petted her and thanked her for never biting us even though we tortured her with costume changes. We thanked her for always being happy to see us when we got home and for being such a wonderful member of our family.

We all began crying, including my dad, as I scooped Pickles up in my arms and carried her to the car. My whole family was standing at the front door crying and holding each other.

I couldn't believe I was the only one willing to do this. It was awful. When I drove away, I looked down at Pickles on the seat and scream-cried the whole way to the vet.

"I'm so sorry, Pickles. I'm so sorry. But you are going to a better place, where you won't be in pain."

I pulled up next to cars at red lights and didn't realize how loud I was scream-crying. People were honking their horns to make sure I was okay.

I pulled up to the vet, scooped up Pickles, and walked in.

Through tears and borderline hyperventilation, I mumbled, "I need to put my dog down."

The vets had me sign some paperwork and told me I could go into the room and say good-bye.

I put my head on top of Pickles. I told her to look out for me in Heaven and to be the guardian angel of our family. I kissed her good-bye and walked out the door.

When my car pulled up in front of my house, I saw my mom come to the front door. I immediately got out and started crying.

"Oh, Jenny, you did the right thing," my mom said.

"No, I didn't," I cried. I opened the back door to my car.

There was Pickles in the backseat.

"I couldn't do it, Mom. I just couldn't do it."

I scooped Pickles up and took her back into the house. Everyone jumped on her crying, happy that we still had Pickles.

We were all so weak it was pathetic.

Poor Pickles.

I prayed that she would die in her sleep, but after three months she was still alive and still peeing and pooing on herself.

Around this time, I started dating a new guy named Donny. He was up to date with what was going on with Pickles because our home stank. One Sunday, he and I were all alone in the house while everyone else was at church and an idea popped into my head.

"Donny, I need you to do me a favor."

"What?"

"Go bring my dog in to be put down."

He looked over at Pickles and back at me. "Are you sure? Don't you want to wait for your family?"

"No. Go now before I change my mind." Once again I burst into tears. I kissed Pickles good-bye and watched Donny carry her to his car.

I felt bad that none of us was going with them, but I had to do something to get her out of the pain she was in and I knew this was the only way.

I ran upstairs to my room and scream-cried into my pillow.

Losing a pet is without a doubt losing a family member, and Pickles will always be remembered as the fifth McCarthy sister.

19

Leap of Faith

I had been home from college for a year and felt really lost. Not having a purpose in life made me feel like a waste. I needed to do something besides work at the Polish grocery store. I was $20,000 in debt and I knew I had to "go big or go home."

I asked myself one simple question: "What do I want to do?"

And then the answer came. I wanted to be Wonder Woman. Not literally, of course (okay, maybe a little) . . . but I wanted to go to Hollywood and host, act, and do something big to help the world like Wonder Woman does.

I picked up the phone book and opened to "commercial agents." (I still can't believe Google didn't exist then.) I landed on an ad for Faces International. It had a picture of a girl who looked like me and the caption said something like, "We take your face to Hollywood." Since I had no idea where else to start, this sounded like a great idea.

I took the bus downtown and headed over to the agency. When I walked in, there were many hopeful Chicagoans sitting in the waiting room primping themselves with the hopes of being plucked out of their suburban lives and asked to move to Hollywood because of their cool face and specialness.

I watched a movie in the waiting room. It was a piece produced by Faces International. It went on to say that one of the last Chicagoans who came from Faces International went on to do a commercial. Then the movie showed a little boy saying, "Yummy!" in front of a bowl of cereal.

I felt like I was in good hands with Faces International. The office looked really professional, so I didn't feel like I was going to be told I needed to sleep with the owner.

"Jenny McCarthy, you're next," said this very sleekly dressed woman.

I sat down next to the woman and she asked about my financial situation. I told her I was $20,000 in debt from college and needed direction on how to go to Hollywood and fulfill my dream.

She said that Faces International charged a fee to put your pictures in the magazine. If I couldn't cover the fee, I wouldn't be able to make it into the magazine's next edition that was going to the top Hollywood casting offices.

"How much is it?" I asked.

"Well, we have to select you for a full page. But you can purchase a half page for $2,500."

"What? I don't have $2,500!"

"Well, I'll put it this way. Think of how much it would cost you to go to Hollywood, plus the cost of getting your headshots done. Faces International will shoot your pictures for you and send them there, and in the meantime you can stay in Chicago."

"But how am I supposed to come up with $2,500?"

"Do you have room on your credit card?"

"I don't have a credit card."

"Well, maybe it's time to get one."

Sadly, I left that bitch's office in search of a credit card. She got to me.

She sold me on the dream and how commercial I looked.

I went to the grocery store and looked for a brochure from a credit card company. I filled one out and prayed to God they would have compassion on my $20,000 college tuition loan.

A few weeks later, my very first credit card came in the mail. It had a $5,000 limit. Credit card companies' favorite people are the ones who are in debt because we can't pay shit off quickly.

My parents had no idea they had just cosigned their credit to me, but I figured I would pay it off right away with my first job.

C *lick, click.*
   I was at my first photo shoot with Faces International. Modeling wasn't something I had ever tried to do, so needless to say, I stood there like I was having my mug shot taken. The photographer tried to get me to relax, but I was having a really hard time.

And then I remembered Ed McMahon. Around this time *Star Search* was on and there was a modeling competition in every show. I could picture the future sluts posing for their modeling round, so I began to imitate them.

"That's it, Jenny," said the photographer. "Now you're getting the hang of it."

I finished the day with a feeling of accomplishment. I felt like I was going to be doing this again.

When I showed the sleekly dressed woman from Faces International my pictures, she *oohed* and *aahed*. I thought my dream of helping my parents someday was about to become a reality.

The sleekly dressed woman said to me, "The owner of Faces International is here. Let's go show him these photos. He's going to be blown away."

We walked down the hallway and entered an even fancier office with an Italian guy who looked like The Situation.

He took a look at my pics and said, "You really got it. We want to choose you for the full page."

I jumped up and down screaming as if Ed McMahon had just told me that I got five stars.

Then he explained that for that full page I had to pay $5,000.

"Five thousand dollars will max out my credit card. I can't."

"You'll get noticed faster with a full page. Trust me. You'll be working in Hollywood in no time."

I was at a crossroads.

I really had no other options at this point and needed to take a leap of faith. I held my breath and handed them my credit card. I prayed to God this was going to work.

When I got home, I watched my mom make dinner for everyone. I watched her cook four things on the stove at the same time. Her hair was disheveled. When I looked down at her feet, I realized that she had been wearing the same gym shoes for at least ten years. She always made sure the needs of her four girls were taken care of before her own. In this moment, watching my mom, I was filled with the most gratitude I had experienced in my life thus far. My heart filled with love and appreciation for this woman who busted her ass to take care of all of us.

As a teenager, I was embarrassed of those gym shoes that she wore; but looking at them in that moment made me want to put them in a shrine.

My mom deserved to be spoiled someday. She deserved really great shoes, and I hoped to God I would help her get them.

Two months later, I was checking the mailbox daily to see if the Faces International casting magazine had arrived. I couldn't wait to see myself in print. I was even more excited to show my parents something good I did. Day after day I waited. Then one day my mom shouted, "Jen, something in the mail came from Faces International."

I ran downstairs from my bedroom, skipping every third step to get there as fast as I could. I turned the corner like the Road Runner and my mom held out an envelope. I grabbed it and walked into the next room.

Once I was alone, I looked down at the envelope and was concerned. This was a normal, letter-size envelope—not a catalog.

I opened the envelope and pulled out a letter. "We are sorry to inform you that Faces International has gone bankrupt and there will be no catalog and no refunds. We apologize."

I fell on the floor.

This couldn't be happening. This was my one shot. I put everything into this. It was my leap of faith. I couldn't believe I had been totally scammed. I felt so stupid. I had charged $5,000 on to my first credit card and had no way of paying it off. I also forged my parents as cosigners, so they would be held accountable if I couldn't pay it. I felt like a lowlife piece of shit. I ran to my room and did my usual scream-cry into the pillow.

✦

20

PRIEST: You Sold Your
Soul to the Devil!

JENNY: And I Gave It to Him
Half Price!

Do you want your milk in a bag?"

The Polish woman wearing a babushka just smiled at me and didn't answer.

That was my signal.

I knew I had to pull out the single Polish sentence that I mastered while working at this mom-and-pop Polish grocery store. It was my one "ta-da!" that really added flair to my job description . . . or so I thought.

"*Chcesz mleka w torebce?*"

"*Tak!*"

I double-bagged the milk because I'm that kind of a person. "*Dziekuja,*" I said, which means "thank you" in Polish.

The woman hobbled out of the store and I was sad to see her go. That was the most excitement I had experienced in four hours. The workday was a slow one.

I plopped on my little stool by the register. I was so bored that I even ran out of daydreams. I would spend hours organizing all the inventory and lining up all the labels. I was like that crazy husband that Julia Roberts tried to escape from in *Sleeping with the Enemy*. Everything was pristine when I was there.

At the grocery, sometimes hours went by with no customers. My eyes would begin to drift down and look at the rack of dirty magazines that we sold. It always grossed me out when someone would buy one. I was such a bitch about it that I would throw the magazine at them instead of putting it in a bag.

But on this excruciatingly slow day, I thought I would take my usual casual peek inside one of the *Playboy* magazines. It was the classiest nudie we sold and didn't show women spreading their legs enough to see their next egg. I looked inside it and thought, *Why couldn't I do this?* The woman I saw in there looked happy as a Playmate and she didn't have that slutty scowl like some other women in other magazines.

I imagined posing for the magazine, accepting my money, and then handing over the naughty little keepsake to my boyfriend, as if it were a personal gift made just for him. Then I envisioned his mother finding it in his bedroom, telling my mother, and then being disowned so quickly I snapped out of my little fantasy and put the magazine away.

I was making $3.75 an hour at the grocery. Paying my college debt off at this rate would take a lifetime. Figuring out a quick way to make cash was in the forefront of my mind daily.

I jumped off my stool, remembering that I hadn't checked my lotto numbers for that week. I pulled out my quick pick and checked the numbers. I sat down to compare them and as I approached the last number, I started to scream. I won one hundred bucks.

Maybe this was a sign. Or a new career path: gambling. I put my ticket in the machine and collected $100.47.

I was alone in the store, so I did a happy dance behind the cash register. I was lost in the moment as I watched myself in the mirror trying to do my best moonwalk.

Then two scary-looking dudes walked in the store. I watched them go in the back and grab some liquor.

I had hoped that was all they wanted, but I had a feeling that something bad was about to happen.

Then the two men walked to the cash register and slammed down the case of beer. My hands started shaking as I fumbled to press the right buttons on the register.

Then, out of the corner of my eye, I saw one of them pull out a gun.

"We'll take everything you got in the register."

My heart started beating out of my chest. I heard a voice in my head that said, "Just stay cool."

I opened the cash register, emptied out everything, and handed it to them.

"You guys got a safe?" they asked.

"I don't know. I'm just the cashier. We get only two customers a day, so I don't think we would have one."

Staring down the barrel of a gun forces your brain to quickly review everything you have and haven't done in your life. Besides not wanting to die because I hadn't accomplished anything yet, I knew that being Catholic and not confessing my sins, especially the big ones in college, meant that I was going to join Satan in Hell. I wasn't about to let that happen.

Then one of the bad guys began to walk around the counter to where I was standing.

I began to shake. He walked in front of me to lift the cash drawer to see if there was any more money hiding there but there wasn't.

The other bad guy started getting agitated. "Come on, man, let's go."

"All right, all right."

The bad guy started walking away from me when he noticed my purse sitting behind the counter. He bent over and picked it up, and the men bolted out of the store.

I stood there in shock.

A customer walked in about a minute later, and all I could do was stand there frozen.

"What aisle are the canned tomatoes in?" she asked.

A tear ran down my cheek.

Words wouldn't come out.

Now that the bad guys were gone, my thoughts didn't consist of "I almost died." They were more along the lines of "Those motherfuckers stole my winning lotto money!"

Once again, I scream-cried into my pillow at home. Nothing seemed to be going right. And to make matters worse, I smelled like Polish sausage.

I fell asleep that night with hopes of finding a way to get to Hollywood and make my parents proud.

. . .

C*lick! Click! Click!*

The next morning, I had JoJo take Polaroid pictures of me next to the garage. We took almost fifty of them.

JoJo was really supportive of my determination to get into show business.

"You look really dumb standing next to the garage door. This is never going to work."

"Well, I don't know what else to do."

"Who are you sending these to anyway?"

"I called the Better Business Bureau to get a list of legitimate agencies and I'm going to mail them out. I'm not getting scammed this time."

"This is really bad. There's chipped paint on the garage door right behind your head, and when you turn around, I can see your bathing suit is going right up your butt."

"Just shut up and do it," I said to her as I self-consciously adjusted my hungry bum.

I mailed Polaroids to about fifty agencies.

A month went by and I heard nothing. I came home day after day still smelling like Polish sausage with absolutely no concept of what my future would look like.

Then one day I heard my mom shout, "Jenny, something came in the mail for you from the Williams Agency."

Again, I bolted down the stairs, skipping every other step, praying that this time it would pay off. I grabbed the letter and secluded myself in the bathroom. Out of fifty pics I sent out, I got one response. *Okay,* I thought. *That's all I needed.* I closed my eyes and prayed, "Please, God, I don't care if this is a small window. I just need You to open it a little. I can squeeze through."

With that I opened the envelope and read the letter.

"Dear Ms. McCarthy, we received your photo and would love to meet you to see if there is a partnership with our agency."

"Oh my God!!!"

I ran out of the bathroom screaming and jumped up and down on every piece of furniture. I forgot to mention that my mom had started nannying babies to bring in extra money for the family, so with every bounce I had to cautiously jump over a sleeping infant. It was like baby hopscotch.

I hugged my mom, kissed her face, and told her that this was all I needed. One chance.

I was going to make it happen.

The morning of the meeting, I decided to borrow something to wear from my friend JCPenney. "Borrowing" is a term we poor but fashionable people use when we buy an outfit, wear it with the tags still on, and then return it the next day. I looked really classy as I rode the hot city bus to downtown Chicago.

(For those of you who read this story in a previous book, I apologize, but it's important and in context to include it in this book too.)

While I rode the bus, I was trying to keep my cool, literally. It was hot and stuffy. I knew ass sweat was building up quickly. As people started getting off at their stops, I became less distracted with my surroundings and more aware of my destination. I started to become self-conscious and imagined myself having to pose in the office for them in my sweaty underwear, so I started to freak out, which made me sweat even more profusely. Thankfully, I always have a spare of clean underwear in my purse in case of emergency, so I figured I could discreetly make a switch. It was now or never. I was a pro at quick wardrobe changes in the back of cars, so I walked to the back row of the bus where it was empty. I could pull this off no problem. Easy and in perfect timing. As I walked up the aisle to get off at my stop, I saw my neighbor Mr. Connors sitting behind the bus driver. He asked me if I was done with the paper. Sure, here you go. I pulled it out and my panties flung with it, straight at him. I was horrified, so I impulsively lied and said, "Those aren't mine!" and ran off the bus.

Hopefully, if he tells his deaf wife, she won't hear him.

I walked into the waiting room of the Williams Agency with my fresh Hanes Her Ways feeling like one hot bitch.

I told them I was there to see Catherine Verrill, and they brought me back to her office. I shook her hand and she asked me what my goals were.

"I would love to do commercial work, act, and host. Not necessarily in that order." I giggled nervously.

"Do you have any more photos of yourself?" she asked.

"I brought some from a photo shoot a couple of months ago." I pulled out my Faces International photos, but I was too scared to tell her where they came from.

"What was this shoot for?" she asked.

"Um . . . for a *Star Search* audition."

Her face started to look perplexed as she scanned my photos and then held one up. "They had you eat an apple while wearing a bikini?"

"I was hungry, and when the photographer caught me eating it, everyone thought it was great."

"Listen, I brought you in here today because I wanted to save you from attempting to get into this business. You don't have a commercial look, and based on that accent, no one will ever let you speak. My advice to you is to get a job bartending downtown. You will have a longer career doing that."

The catatonic look returned. At this point in my life, I had it mastered.

I couldn't believe this woman was shamelessly destroying my attempt to get into the business.

My eyes filled with tears as I leaned into her desk. "That's not a very nice thing to say," I told her. "Shitting on people's dreams is like telling a child that Santa isn't real and then laughing at them. I'll be sure to send you an autographed copy of my major magazine cover."

I grabbed my photos and stormed out of her office. When I made it to the curb, my body collapsed and I broke into tears.

I didn't know what the hell I was going to do. And to make matters worse, the price tag had fallen off my outfit.

While wiping the tears off my face, I noticed the building across the street. It had the Playboy icon on it. My thoughts flashed to the *Playboy* magazines in the Polish grocery store and I wondered why I couldn't do it.

Then my thoughts flashed on my mom shaking her head and sobbing hysterically as she began to drown in her tears of shame.

But I guess my body didn't care because I found myself walking across the street to enter the Playboy Building.

Once inside, I inquired at the desk about how girls become Playmates. The receptionist dismissed me and told me that no one ever just walks in. You have to submit photos. As I walked back toward the elevator, I decided to surrender my dream and not try anymore.

I was done.

I was going to look for a husband, have babies, and hope I could help my parents out financially in other ways.

"Excuse me. Are you here to inquire about being a Playmate?"

I turned around and saw a man in a suit who obviously worked there.

"Yes," my mouth said.

"My photographer is doing a shoot back there. Why don't you come back and slip into a bikini and we'll submit you?"

My heart was racing.

This was it.

Do I sell my soul to the devil or let go of my dream?

There must have been two devils on my shoulder that stabbed their little pitchforks into the angel and swung him off my body, because I started to follow the photographer as he led me to a dressing room. I looked down at myself as I took off my clothes and put on a skimpy bikini.

When I turned to look in the mirror, I was horrified to see my incredibly hairy bush sticking out of the bikini from every angle. I had never shaved or trimmed down there before. I blamed it on the two-sizes-too-small bikini bottom. I then politely asked for a medium size and successfully covered my roadkill crotch.

Pose. *Click!* Pose. *Click!*

On the city bus headed back home, I was so depressed that I was hoping the bus would get into an accident, and I would fly through the window.

By the time I got home, I had received a call on my answering machine.

"Hi, Jenny. We want you to officially test to be Miss October. Please call us back to set up a shoot. You will be offered twenty thousand dollars if you accept."

I had never been so excited and horrified all at the same time. It was like getting news that your grandpa died but he left you $20 million. My sister Lynette came into my room and I shared the news with her.

"Can you keep a secret?"

"Yeah, okay."

"I just got called by *Playboy* to be Miss October."

"What?! You can't do that. Mom and Dad will kill you. I mean kill you kill you."

"I don't have any other choice, Lynette. They are paying twenty thousand dollars! That will pay off my school loan and get me to Hollywood."

"Oh, God. I'm scared for you."

I was scared for me too. I came up with a plan to take $2,000 out of my paycheck and send my parents on a cruise the week the issue came out to avoid any backlash. That by far was the smartest thing I had ever done in my life.

The October issue came out. My parents were in the Caribbean when I answered our kitchen phone.

"Hello."

"Who is this?"

"It's Jenny."

"*What in God's name is wrong with you?* You have completely disgraced the family. This is your uncle Ken."

My heart sank and my legs collapsed and turned into jelly. This had been one of my favorite uncles.

"Why would you sell your soul to the devil?"

"I want to get to Hollywood. I want to make a career for myself and take care of my parents someday."

"You will never get a career from this. I'm ashamed. And your parents will never accept your evil money." He slammed the phone down.

Once again, I sat in my kitchen in a catatonic state. Just when I started to feel like my plan was going to work, I became frozen with fear.

When my parents returned from their vacation, I wasn't there to absorb the volcano. Playboy had me in San Diego doing an appearance.

Lynette had my back and handed Mom and Dad the letters I wrote to each of them.

My mom did exactly what I expected.

She had a nervous breakdown.

I felt horrible.

She refused to speak to me for three days.

When I finally got her on the phone, she was crying. "What are people going to think? I didn't raise you to do something like this!"

"Mom, I'm sorry, but I know deep down inside I'm going to

make it in Hollywood. I'm going to do something good. I just needed a way in."

We cried on the phone together for hours.

Eventually, my mom said, "Well, you're my daughter and I love you. I'm going to stick by you and trust you."

That's all I needed to hear.

I was going to make my mom proud.

A few months later, my parents and I received a letter from a cousin who was a priest.

He said that my soul was damned to Hell.

He also said that if I didn't go to the media and beg for God's forgiveness, my family would be excommunicated.

I was so angry. I couldn't understand how judgmental and evil someone from my family—a priest—could be.

This was the fuel I needed to prove everyone wrong. But first I needed to figure out a way to help my family move out of our shitty neighborhood and pay off the debts they had accumulated over the years. And there was one way to make that happen: Playmate of the Year. I was already convinced at this point I was going to Hell, so I figured why not make the best of it and walk all the way into the fire?

Six months later, I came back to Chicago to visit my mom and dad.

I had been living in Los Angeles all these months and wanted to take them out to dinner. I chose a restaurant in our neighborhood that we always drove past but never went into because we couldn't afford it. While we enjoyed our filet mignon, my mom reminisced about all the people in the neighborhood who were still very upset about my being in *Playboy*. She ended it with, "I'm just so glad this is behind us and you didn't win that Playmate of the Year thing."

I chugged my wine and responded, "That's why we're eating filet mignon."

My mom slowly lowered her fork. "What do you mean?" she said.

My dad followed with "You won?"

Again, I had never been so excited and horrified at the same time. "Yes, I won one hundred thousand dollars, and I just paid off every one of your credit cards and loans, and I want you to move out of the house."

My mom and dad exhaled deeply. I could tell they were experiencing the same emotions I had felt: happiness and terror.

"I remember when we thought we won the McDonald's Monopoly game," I said. "It killed me to see you both so excited and then so disappointed. I've waited for this day to happen since then. I promise you both that I plan on doing good with this opportunity. I'm going to make you both so proud."

I flew back to California with an amazing feeling of accomplishment. I took care of my parents just like I had always wanted to, and now it was time to take care of myself.

The only problem was that after paying my parents' bills, I was back to zero. I was completely broke. But I had faith that I would come back strong.

After all, my hero was Wonder Woman, and that bitch always made shit happen.

me in my new role as Bunny

21

I'm Losing My Religion . . .
Just Like R.E.M.

When I moved to Los Angeles in 1993, I had hoped that it wouldn't be that bad of a place. After all, the English translation means "the Angels." That had to be a blessing!

I was sure I would find a group of friends who were good people and would guide me in the right direction. I just wasn't sure how to find them.

What if I was like Sandy in *Grease* and befriended a gang of girls who weren't really nice and forced me to perm my hair?

Down the street from my new apartment there was a laundromat. From my kitchen window, I could see people coming and going with their baskets.

The laundromat wasn't an ideal place to meet new friends, but it was the only place I really "hung out" at frequently.

Like clockwork, every Wednesday night I would grab my basket of clothes and head down there with a couple of magazines. It was never really the same group of people, and aside from small talk, I never made any connections with anyone or really hit it off.

I guess my fantasy of meeting my dream man at the laundromat was a little off.

There was a man who always went at the same time as me and I never had a good feeling about him.

He introduced himself as Christopher and looked to be in his late thirties. He always appeared disheveled like he had just eaten at a greasy spoon and used his top as a napkin. He would park himself in the chair next to me no matter where he was already stationed.

"Do you need some quarters?" he would ask in the most nasal-sounding Kermit the Frog voice.

"No, I don't, thanks," I would respond without making much eye contact.

After some time, I would come home and realize that a bra was missing. Another time a silky G-string was gone. My black thong, vanished. Did the sock monster have a relative? Sometimes I would throw my stuff into the dryer, grab a coffee next door, and then come back.

Ahhhh. I was starting to put the two together. Christopher was a perverted panty thief! I had to catch him in the act.

The following Wednesday, Christopher was at the laundromat, like always. He moved to the chair next to my station, as usual. I took out my clothes from the washer and threw them into the dryer and stepped outside to grab my pretend coffee. I waited a minute to give him time to repeat-offend, then I walked back into the laundromat and saw Christopher shove my thong into his pants and start jerking off.

"What the fuck!?" was all I could say. The three other people in the laundromat turned around, obviously alarmed from the shrill in my voice.

"This creep is rubbing my thong on his dick!"

A guy in his twenties that I nicknamed Superman immediately came to the rescue and put him in a headlock. "Give her her panties back, loser."

Before I could say, "No, I don't want them!" Superman yanked Christopher's pants down and exposed his little Tic Tac.

When he bent over to pick up his pants, I saw the gold cross around his neck swing like a pendulum. This man was religious?

With all the temptations that existed in the world, Christopher had to victimize me? I wanted to tear the rosary off his neck and choke him with my Wonderbra, but instead I just walked away feeling violated by a man who clearly disobeys God. Christopher was definitely going to Hell. I left and vowed to never return to that laundromat again.

But the laundromat was a stone's throw away from a bookstore called the Psychic Eye Book Shop that kept winking at my soul. Every time I would drive past it, I kept saying, "I gotta go in there."

Shit like that always looked so interesting to me because I was fascinated with reading minds, and considering that my intuition had always been one of my best assets—well, I actually listened to it.

One day, I took a stroll into the Psychic Eye and instantly felt a sense of belonging. The smell of incense, the music of monks chanting, and the cool hippies—they all felt strangely familiar to me.

I ran my fingers past some books and let my energy pick the

one that felt right. I landed on one called *Spiritual Growth: Being Your Higher Self.* The summary said the book offers the next step in spiritual growth for those who want to know who they are and why they are here on Earth. *Holy shitballs*, I thought. That was me they were talking about. Just like in the movie *The Jerk* when Steve Martin finds his special purpose, I felt this was the answer to my spiritual evolution. Catholicism wasn't helping me evolve anymore, so the idea of this felt fresh and exciting.

I wasn't losing my religion at this point. I was just opening my mind to learning different belief systems.

On my walk home, carrying my new book, all I could think about were those two sentences.

Who am I?

Why am I here?

I think these are common questions for anyone in their twenties. Although I do know many sixty-year-olds who are still asking those same questions.

I ran up to my apartment and dove into the book. I was devouring the pages like chocolate. There were no abstract mythical stories like those in the Bible. I wasn't feeling fear or any wrath of God. Instead, I was feeling inspired, empowered, and awakened.

This was 1993. There wasn't a boom yet of spiritually enlightening books like *The Power of Now*, but this book was shifting my twenty-one-year-old spirit more than any of Oprah's "Aha!" moments ever could.

One of the biggest holy shits for me was the realization that I was in control of my own destiny.

The book explained that when we connect to our higher selves, we can make anything we want happen. It talked about raising your vibration. At first I wasn't sure what that meant. Did I need stronger batteries for my vibrator?

I continued reading as it described the energy field we all have around our bodies called an aura.

Being fresh out of eighteen years of Bible study, it took me a while to wrap my head around the idea of this aura, but it felt right.

I started to practice expanding my energy field and bringing it back in. I would try to connect with my higher self. All that really means is being awake—dropping the illusions and stories we walk around with every day and looking at people with love and truth. This awakening hit me so hard that I couldn't talk to any friends for a few weeks. I sat in it night after night, opening my mind, which was then opening my heart.

I would giggle to myself, knowing there was a whole new world out there that didn't involve shame and guilt.

At the age of twenty-one, I found myself turning down LA parties to sit on the floor of the Psychic Eye Book Shop on Friday nights. I couldn't have been happier. With every book I read, the fear of becoming trapped in Satan's lair was becoming less realistic. Especially after reading almost thirty books about people who had had near-death experiences. They had the most incredibly beautiful stories of Heaven. Real assholes and perverts like Christopher who had near-death experiences talked about how great Heaven was. If they could get there, so could I.

During this spiritual transformation, I continued to attend church every Sunday. But church wasn't giving me the high I received from the spiritual books that were empowering me.

As I sat there one Sunday staring at the priest, I tried to actually pay attention to the Mass. I had always just gone to church to not break a commandment, but now I thought, *What the hell? Let me hear what the old bird is saying.*

What did I get out of it? Absolutely nothing. I felt good during some of the singing, but the overall feeling in the room was about guilt and seeking redemption. To me, it was like buying a product I wasn't confident with and then being stuck with it. There is no exchange or return policy and there is certainly no explanation as to why it may not be working for you. It just has to, so don't question the mechanics of it. As a "buyer," there's a hell of a lot of remorse, and I was being reminded of that.

What I did like about church was that it was a place that held me accountable for my actions.

But the problem was that I was being held accountable for all of my negative actions. I wanted a place that held me accountable for my positive ones too.

As Catholics, we sort of collect sins like food at a grocery store. We throw them into the cart, then we go to church and look at all those sins in the basket and beg for forgiveness.

I was tired of focusing each week on the bad things that I had done. It was such a negative space and seemed to attract only more negativity and more sins.

I tried to talk to my new LA friends about this, but they thought this path I was on was crazy. They said I looked so peaceful all the time that it became annoying to them. They were especially upset that nothing pissed me off anymore. They wanted to gossip and get mad at people, and I would giggle about it, knowing that any daggers they were throwing at others were being thrown back at themselves.

Slowly, I started to notice my friendships dissipate, and I found myself more and more alone. I was a Playboy Playmate at this time, so you would think I would be caught up in orgies and parties (don't worry, I am in future chapters), but in this initial awakening I was very alone.

I have no doubt that I was operating on a really high vibration. The best way to describe it now was like I was on satellite radio and everyone around me was still on AM.

I had to figure out what to do—either continue on this path of spiritual awakening by myself or go back to the static frequency and wait for some friends to catch up to me.

I watched from the outside as the world walked by, including Christopher coming out of the laundromat with his hamper, and I wondered whom he victimized this time.

I sat alone in my apartment and lowered my frequency to fit in with my friends. I felt a downshift inside me and hoped one day I would make it back to satellite radio.

22

I See Dead People

I had always believed that there were people on Earth who were able to see ghosts, but I was never one of them until the night I pounded five hits of Ecstasy.

Playboy had a group of girls going to Hawaii to shoot a video of them doing competitive water sports. They hired me as the host, which meant that I didn't have to jet ski topless. Off we went to Maui to have an amazing time being young and stupid and (for the rest of the girls) naked.

On our last day there, the production team decided to host a luau, where we caught many people's eyes on the beach—probably because we looked like a lost episode of *Baywatch*. Suddenly, out of the water emerged this gorgeous hunk of a man. If you saw the movie *Couples Retreat*, he would have been the hot yoga teacher who molests all the wives.

He sauntered over to us girls, who had seen only large Samoan people all week, and he had a smile that made our vaginas start clapping.

He told us all about this private beach we could meet him at later and spend the night on. It was our last night there, so we figured why not?

There was a full moon that night, which only accentuated the craziness that was about to unfold. We made it to the beach, and again our hot man emerged out of the water looking like some mystical merman. He grabbed a towel from inside his bag that was next to us, and we watched him dry off his hard, shredded body. Then he reached inside his bag once more and held up a little black box like it was magic.

I was really hoping it wasn't a glow-in-the-dark condom. I had seen one too many of those in 1994.

"I brought some Ecstasy!" he said.

Uh-oh. I had never done it before.

No one else seemed to be too concerned, though. Holding up drugs in front of a group of Playmates was like holding up an arm to a cannibal tribe.

We jumped on the box, fighting to get as many little white capsules as possible.

Instead of saving some for later, we all pounded at least five at once. For anyone who has done E before, I know what you just said.

Holy shitballs! No, she didn't!

Yes, I did. And so did the other geniuses I was with.

We hung out on the beach waiting for something to kick in.

Just when I started to believe we were given Tylenol instead of Ecstasy, my skin began melting into the sand. I was amazed by how the sand felt under my toes. It felt like I was walking on warm marshmallows.

"Come here! These marshmallows aren't sticky!" I shouted excitedly as if I had discovered a new planet. Metaphorically, I was traveling in another galaxy.

I ran over to two of my girlfriends and yanked on their arms to get them up. "Come on, bitches! Get up!"

But when my friends turned into old ladies, I screamed and backed away, tripping on tree branches as I watched the old ladies then turn into rocks.

Strange things were happening. Everything was suddenly extra peachy and dreamlike.

The looks on the girls' faces were filled with such happiness. Even though I didn't know some of these girls' names, I felt driven to tell them what beautiful beings they were. So I walked on the water (much like Jesus did) and began to speak (much like Jesus did). "My children, I love you all so deeply. You are such beautiful beings."

"We love you so much too."

I looked at Miss December and said, "I can finally see your spirit and it's beautiful. You're not the cunt I thought you were at all."

She smiled back.

"That is so nice of you! Thank you so much."

While we continued to talk about how much we loved each other, I noticed we were all rubbing each other's heads, giving intense skull massages. It felt freaking awesome.

The moon was full and the air was warm as we continued riding our head-rubbing train with limbs entangled, sitting waist-deep in the ocean.

Waves of deep sensory stimulations went through my body. It was incredibly intense. So much so that we all began to express our love for one another by making out with each other. It was beyond ridiculous, but we were no longer in control of our actions.

I looked around and I saw our hot surfer man standing about fifty feet away from us with his mouth hanging open.

I can only imagine the shock he was in seeing that he was the only man on the beach with fourteen really fucked-up Playmates who just happened to also be making out with each other.

Once that initial wave of sexual intensity calmed down, we tried to focus, but our eyeballs kept wanting to flip back into our heads.

Surfer man started to approach us, but the look on his face had changed from shocked hotness to Hannibal Lecter.

I whispered to the girls through my chattering teeth, "Hey, you guys, he's walking toward us and I think he wants to eat us for dinner."

"Holy shit. It's true!" cried Miss December. "He has forks in his eyes!"

All the girls looked at him and moved in closer to form a tight cuddle puddle. "Hey, beautiful ladies, you're looking delicious."

I'm sure he meant nothing by his comment, but one can't be so sure when you're on drugs on a deserted beach with a stranger, so I thought I would lead the group with my response. "Run!"

I had no idea where I was going, but all the girls seemed to be following me. Once I thought we were far enough away, I jumped behind a big bush. (No, it wasn't Miss December's.) All I knew was that if we took five hits of E, we were probably in for many more, bigger waves of this shit.

I sat up and tried to give the girls a pep talk for the sake of our survival. "You guys, um, we're fucked," I said. It wasn't exactly the pep talk I was hoping for. Just then I noticed that we weren't wearing anything. "Um, and we're fucking naked."

"No, I'm wearing a bikini," said Miss November.

"Um, no, you're not. You're hallucinating."

Miss February chattered, "What the hell do we do now?" They all looked at me like I was the sober, logical one, when in fact I was the sole cause of the paranoid state everyone was in.

Miss May said, "Let's just walk to the nearest freeway and get help."

I responded, "Um, no, let's not. We're fucking naked. Let's just try to sneak back to the beach and get our clothes."

With that, another wave of Ecstasy hit.

I found myself holding a tree to brace myself. The texture felt so good that I decided to rub my head and boobs all over it. I noticed I was moaning loudly, which snapped me back to reality. I was shocked when I realized I wasn't rubbing on a tree—I was rubbing on Miss June!

"Holy shit, I'm sorry. I thought you were a tree."

Then Miss June walked up behind me and said, "Who are you talking to?"

I looked back. It *was* a tree I was humping.

"Fuck," I said. "I am fucked up, you guys."

I looked around at the other girls, who were either spinning in circles or also humping trees. "Come on, let's keep going."

This must have been an act of God to punish me. I heard a chanting voice breathing down my neck.

"Bimbos in limbo."

I wondered how many bugs we were walking on with our bare feet. I was still the leader of the idiots, so I was doing my best to try to stay calm. Just then, I froze in my tracks when I noticed a man wearing pioneer clothing from the nineteenth century standing in front of me, holding a bouncing baby up to me.

One of the Playmates said, "Why did you stop?"

I whispered, "There's a guy from the 1800s holding up his baby to me right now. I think he wants me to take his baby."

Miss December looked at me like I was fucking crazy.

"Listen, bitch, there is a guy standing here looking like he was shipwrecked or something and I think he wants me to rescue his kid."

Miss September shouted to the other girls, "You guys, Jenny is really, really fucked up. I think we need to help her."

"Jenny, there is nothing there."

All the girls joined me and we stood there in silence until I heard Miss March yell, "Holy shit, there is a guy standing there holding his baby to us."

Suddenly, they were all seeing the man with the same exact description.

Miss July shouted, "The baby is wearing a white dress!"

Then I knew we were all seeing the same freaking thing.

Miss December asked, "Should we try to talk to it?"

"They're dead," I said.

"Well, if they're dead, why is he holding his baby up to us?"

"I don't know. Maybe tell them to go to the light or something."

"Go to the light! Go to the light!" she shouted. "You would think his arms would be tired from holding the baby up so long."

"Let's just go," I said. "I'm so freaked out." We all began to walk away when suddenly we were surrounded by about sixty different kinds of dead people.

"What the fuck is happening?" shouted Miss June.

I responded, "Um, you guys are seeing this too, right?"

"Yes!" they all shouted. All the dead people looked as if they had been shipwrecked.

Now imagine fourteen Playmates holding on to one another for dear life walking naked through a Hawaiian jungle. "You guys, I'm sure we're almost done tripping our balls off." I was trying to calm them down. "I feel like we've been on this for fifteen hours."

One of the girls looked at her watch and said, "It's been only twenty minutes."

"What?!" I shouted.

I couldn't even imagine what would happen to us two hours from then when in twenty minutes I had had sex with a tree and was seeing dead people.

I figured if we just kept walking, we were bound to walk into something. And something was exactly what we walked into. Something really, really bad and totally fucking insane.

Slowly, we lifted our heads to take in the sight that stood before us.

Standing in front of us was a fifty-foot Grim Reaper.

I wondered, "Did we die in the bush back there, or did Hannibal kill us on the beach? Is that why we're seeing dead people, because we're part of them?"

Miss December whispered, "I think I just peed."

Miss July responded, "No, I just peed on you. I'm so scared."

I looked over at my friends to grab one of their hands and run for it but saw them lying lifeless sprawled all over the beach.

I rubbed my eyes and opened them. This time, to my horror, their limbs were detached and strewn all over the beach, legs sticking up in the sand and boobs floating in the ocean.

I rubbed my eyes again and my friends ran past me at full speed, screaming for their lives, boobs jiggling everywhere. It was starting to feel like a National Lampoon version of Michael Jackson's "Thriller."

I was still frozen. I stood dead-on face-to-face with this fucking crazy thing. I remember thinking, *It's obviously dark and evil, so the best thing I can do is scream the Our Father prayer.*

I immediately started to scream the Our Father as loud as I could and with the strongest belief in God I could muster to make this thing go away. About halfway through the prayer, poof, it was gone.

And so were my friends.

The two issues I was having at this point were insane dehydration and the man with his baby still fucking following me. I kept turning around and yelling, "Go to the light!"

If you thought my basement was scary, this shit in the jungle was epic. I couldn't wait to tell JoJo!

When I got to the beach, a few girls were there sitting by the water still holding on to each other and another two were scissoring. I was able to see now and they all looked pretty awful, like they had stumbled home from a monthlong walk of shame and were out of their minds.

"Where is Hannibal Lecter?" I asked.

"We have no idea."

I sat down next to them, and when I turned my head to the right, I realized a chubby Hawaiian ghost was sitting right next to me.

"Do you guys see this chubby Hawaiian guy sitting next to me right now?"

They leaned forward and looked.

"Yup."

He didn't seem to be bothering us, so I let him sit next to me. But when the dead guy holding his baby showed up on the beach again, I had just about had it. I stood up, trying to balance with my legs crossed and my hands covering my nipples. The other girls became self-aware and immediately crossed their legs and cupped their boobs too.

Miss June fell over, tits up.

"Dude, we are cracked out of our minds, so please stop looking at us like that and stop holding up your baby to us like we are supposed to do something with it. Go to the light like Carol Anne did."

The dead guy holding the baby still wouldn't leave.

"Let's try to get back to our hotel. It's only a matter of time before every dead ghost on this island finds us, and I don't think I can handle the Grim Reaper again."

Miss December then shouted out her brilliant idea. "What if we waved down a boat to take us back to the United States?"

After we walked for what felt like four hours but turned out to be ten minutes, I saw what looked like a street next to the beach up ahead.

Miss February walked over to it and touched it. "It feels like a street."

"Thank God, it's a street! Let's follow the road because all the hotels are pretty much on one street."

Just as we were about to transition into a new setting (meaning the street), another wave of E hit us, causing all of us to lie down immediately.

I was looking up into the sky, thinking now about how fucking amazing I felt. I couldn't stop chewing on my cheeks for some reason. It felt so good.

The stars looked like they were right in front of me. Just as I thought I actually might touch a star, dead man holding the baby blocked my view.

"Aw, dude, please. Just fuck off. Or go follow Miss June. I think she likes you."

I tried to tune in to my third eye to see if he was trying to telepathically say anything. All I picked up was "Please take my baby."

If ghosts are real, then this was pretty sad. I'm not sure why he didn't go to the light with his baby when he died, but he was really barking up the wrong set of trees with this group.

Even though we all felt as if we had lost the ability to stand, I knew we had to keep moving. We all held on to one another as we made our way down the street.

Then Miss June grabbed my shoulder and turned me around. "Look, I have knees!" she said, pointing at them.

"Oh my God, so do I. But mine can't move," Miss July said with a surprised look as she lifted her stiff leg to demonstrate her disability.

"We all have knees, you moron," said Miss December as she kicked the back of Miss July's legs, causing them to bend.

I guessed that Miss December was the most sober because I was just about to join in on the knee discovery myself.

As we walked, all the girls, including myself, after regaining the ability to use our legs (and knees, apparently), suddenly lost the ability to speak. We couldn't form a sentence if we tried.

Miraculously, though, we made it back to our condo. I don't know how, but we eventually walked all the way there.

I woke up the next day feeling awful.

To make matters worse, I had chewed the insides of my mouth so bad that I had about seventeen canker sores, and when I got home, my boyfriend thought I had acquired an STD.

I was so completely freaked out by this experience that I had trouble sleeping alone for years.

Even today, as I type this book in my dark bedroom, I can't help but think that maybe the dead man holding the baby is standing next to me.

Eek! Go to the light!

my first mug shot into Hell

23

There Is Only So Much Bleach a Girl Can Take

My reign of Playmate of the Year 1994 was coming to a close. I was excited to finally be able to go from forty-volume bleach to twenty-volume bleach. I had fun on tour, but I was ready to evolve past the superficially sexy persona I was forced to portray.

But first, I had a few more dinners to attend as PMOY. Usually these dinners consisted of men who were "distributors" of the magazine in other countries. And time and time again I had to listen to the same crap that came out of their mouths.

"My wife ignores me."

To which I had no problem replying, "Well, maybe she's upset about something you're doing or not doing."

One dork replied with a thick French accent, "I do nothing wrong. I take good care of her. I don't know what else I could do."

I replied with a thick American accent, "Well, for starters, why don't you take your hand off my fucking knee and sleep in *her* bed tonight?"

I finally had to come up with a creative way to keep these men from hitting on me at those dinners. It would make me so incredibly sad to watch their pathetic egos try to woo us Playmates while their wives were at home working hard to raise their kids. Somebody had to be out in the war zone defending these women. I knew I would want the same. So at the next dinner I had to attend, I came up with a plan that would no doubt turn these boys off.

I was told to sit between Receding Hair and Lazy Eye. So I bunny-hopped to my seat and shook hands with both of them. They always smelled the same (kind of like bologna) and had the same leering look in their eye, which made me want to puke up my lunch on their heads.

"Hello, hello!" Receding Hair said.

"Hi!" I responded like a sweet, innocent bunny. Then I turned to my right and put out my paw. "Hi, what's your name?"

"Frank. My name is Frank. It's very nice to meet you. You are very beautiful." He then tickled my paw with his finger much like one does in eighth grade.

I did a fake giggle while holding on to his hand and turned it over to purposely call out his wedding ring. "Wow, that's a beautiful wedding band. Is your wife's band just as beautiful?"

Lazy Eye Frank replied, "Um . . . uh . . . yeah."

I was on a mission. I wanted to make these men pay for their sins.

Mind you, we Playmates weren't helping the situation by being there dressed to the nines. We were like pieces of chocolate to a table full of PMSing women.

Then I felt a nudge on my leg from Receding Hair Man, which was quickly followed with a hand trying to go up my skirt.

I'm not exaggerating. This actually happened a lot. Some girls didn't mind. I minded. I minded all the time and didn't put up with it. I had so much self-worth set in me at a young age, and I thank my parents every day for it. Otherwise, I would have had Receding Hair performing a body cavity search on me at this dinner.

Instead, I quickly kicked Receding Hair's hand away and decided to utilize my weapon of mass destruction that I came up with in order to get these men to stop their sexual assaults.

I leaned over to Receding Hair and said, "Do you want to know what makes me so happy?"

"Diamonds?" he replied.

"No, silly. . . . What makes me happy is Jesus," I said in the most upbeat Christian voice. "Ever since I accepted Jesus Christ as my Lord and savior, my life has become blissful."

The look on his face was like watching an inflatable balloon lose all of its air. His "I might get pussy tonight" smile quickly turned into a foul grimace. The best way to describe it is the look on your husband's face when you farted in your ninth month of pregnancy: shocked and grossed out.

My weapon of mass destruction worked.

And, I proved that Jesus is *not* an aphrodisiac.

Receding Hair turned the other direction, locked eyes with Miss May's ass and quickly made his way over to her like she was turkey on Thanksgiving.

I didn't waste a beat. I turned to my right to work on Frank and his lazy eye.

"So, Frank, have you ever experienced love on a level that makes your entire body tremble with joy?"

Frank's smile grew and the eyebrow above his lazy eye pointed up to the heavens. "Are you asking me about making love?" he asked.

"No, Frank. I'm asking you about a love that is so deep and great that if you had it in your heart, you would never have to look elsewhere for gratification again."

"Wow," he replied. "Where can I get some of that?"

"You can find it in Jesus and in His Father. I'm sure you've heard of him before. He sometimes goes by The Creator."

Frank sat in silence. For the first time that night, he was looking at my eyes and not my cleavage. I decided to pound him into the ground with some more verbiage.

"Even though Jesus is all-forgiving, I don't think your wife would be as understanding that you are trying to seduce a girl thirty years younger than you."

"Did my wife hire you to spy on me?"

"No, Frank. I work for Jesus."

He stood up, threw his napkin down, and walked to the bar.

Mission accomplished. Who knew Jesus was such a great cockblock?

As the months went on, I broke two men's noses with my right hook and got one guy fired from his job. It was clearly time for me to go through my own metamorphosis and trade in my bunny ears for wings. So I closed my eyes and made a wish. (After years of reading spiritual books, I have come to realize those wishing moments were actually me putting out an intention. Oprah would have been proud.)

I made an intention to find a job that would allow me to show all of my colors. I wanted to be my real, funny, down-to-earth, goofy self. I wanted to break the mold of the sexy stereotype. I knew being sexy had a shelf life of twenty years in Hollywood (if you're lucky), and I knew I was more than implants.

As serendipity would have it, I found out that MTV was having an audition for hosts for a new dating show called *Singled Out*. I couldn't think of a better job that would allow me to be all of the things I wanted to be. I asked my manager to call and get me into the audition. I had a good feeling about this, but I needed to get in the door. When my manager called me back, he said MTV told him that there wasn't a chance in hell they would ever hire a Playmate.

I couldn't believe it. I couldn't understand how they wouldn't at least let me give it a shot. So I took matters into my own hands and crashed the audition under an alias. I was determined to show them that there *was* a chance in hell they could hire me and I was worthy of this job.

By the time the fifteenth callback happened, I was outed. They knew I was that Playmate who wanted to audition weeks prior.

Fortunately, as time passed, MTV saw that not only was I capable of the job, but I did a great job portraying myself as a self-deprecating, psychotic cheerleader who knew how to control horny men while always rooting for the girls. Something, ironically, that I learned while touring for Playboy.

On the seventeenth callback, I got the job. I couldn't believe it. I called my mom and told her the great news.

"Mom, I did it! I got a job on MTV!"

"I don't know what that is. I don't understand why you don't just take Vanna White's job."

God bless my mother, but I knew that this self-deprecating, psychotic cheerleader was ready to come out blazing and would soon gross out men all over America.

I was tired of being one-dimensional. I wanted to fart and pick my nose while wearing hot pants. I wanted to confuse the masses— especially men. I wanted to introduce them to a new female kind of thinking called "I don't give a shit what you think."

I guess it worked, because halfway through the first season of *Singled Out*, men were coming up to me telling me I was too hot to be so disgusting and I needed to stick to just being sexy because it was confusing their brains and their masturbation sessions.

By far, this is one of the best compliments I have ever received in show business. I knew that somehow, I was changing the way that women wanted to be perceived. I was leading a charge of women who hoped to prove that we can stink up a bathroom just as much as men can.

✦

24

Oh No, My Mom
Is Going to Hell!

My mom and dad got divorced when I was twenty-three. Of course it was difficult on me considering how hard I worked to make sure that they were happy, but what I would soon come to realize is that sometimes divorce can make people even happier. Twelve years ago, my mom reconnected with and remarried her high-school sweetheart, a man named Tom. They love each other deeply but have never been able to fully experience utopia because of the difficulties they have gone through to stay devout Catholics after their respective divorces.

Let me explain this insanity:

The Catholic Church says that if you are a divorced Catholic, you are living in sin and are therefore not permitted to go to communion. As a Catholic, one of the requirements to avoid excommunication is to go to confession and communion once a year. Well, if you're a divorced Catholic and can't go to communion, after your first year of divorce, you are automatically excommunicated. This also means, of course, that you're living in sin and will go to Hell when you die. However, there is a loophole, which states that whichever spouse dies last gets to go to Heaven again.

These are rules according to the Catholic Church.

Shocking, stupid, and true.

How they can throw my mom, my stepdad, and my dad in Hell with Hitler makes me want to protest outside the Vatican. My mom and stepdad have never missed one Sunday Mass, and both have to sit and watch everyone in the church take communion while they sit there thinking about what Hell will be like for them. I'm sure sometimes they are also praying that their exes run into the Grim Reaper before they do so they can ensure anew their tickets to Heaven.

After years of watching my parents' struggle to remain devout Catholics, I decided to intervene and buy them a book for Christmas that I thought could help them.

It is called *All Lutherans Go to Heaven.*

Tom and Mom at their high school prom

25

Belly Cries to *Belly Laughs*

After watching a horrific, circa 1970 child-birthing video during Sex Ed in seventh grade, I never in a million years could have believed I would be capable of delivering a baby. I was also scared by the enormous amount of pubes that woman had in the video. Don't get me wrong—I'm known for my fair share of roadkill pussy, but this woman had an ape between her legs, not a squirrel.

I also had no idea vaginas could open up like that. Too bad penises couldn't expand.

My pregnancy was nothing short of happy hell. Happy because I was pregnant, and hell because I seemed to experience every symptom I had ever read about, plus a plethora of bizarre ones that are never mentioned in the typical pregnancy books.

My hormones were so out of control that a day didn't go by where I didn't want to destroy my husband. I cried, threw remote controls at him, made him change the TV station if a Victoria's Secret commercial was on, ordered him to run out for food that looked good on TV, and then made him live through the worst pregnancy farts known to mankind.

I have no doubt a lot of my stress stemmed not only from my body morphing into a house, but also the fact that I was the only breadwinner in the family. My ex hates when I talk about this, but it's reality. Most people get to tell everyone they know they are pregnant. I had to hide it like I was giving birth to the Messiah because I feared I would be considered disabled in show business.

Plus, at this point, my career was like a plane delayed on a runway. I was twenty-nine years old and for four years I had been in holding deals. What that means is a network puts a hold on actors it likes, but by doing so, the actors are not allowed to do anything else. I was stuck in this cycle of being paid a little bit to sit and do nothing until a network figured out what to do with me. This might sound amazing to some people, but I knew that sitting around unable to work was only sending my career into no-man's-land. People were coming up to me on the street asking, "Did you quit show business?" This was hard to hear, and it was impossible to explain that I was stuck in a vicious cycle of holding deals.

Then it finally happened. A network figured out how to utilize me.

There was a pilot that I was elated to do, except it required me to wear sexy, tiny clothes. Normally I would be fine with that, but there was a little problem. I was five months pregnant. I knew if the network knew I was pregnant, I wouldn't be able to do the TV show and the network would most likely cut me loose from the holding deal. There was no way I could survive financially without doing the pilot.

Two weeks before filming, word got out that I was pregnant and my biggest fear came true. I was let go from my holding deal and not allowed to do the pilot because I was pregnant. They actually told my lawyer I was disabled. My lawyer then explained to me that I could sue the shit out of them—but my chances of ever working again would be slim to none if I went through with it. The moment I got that phone call, I burst into tears and went into premature labor. I was rushed to the hospital and told that I was indeed in labor (in my fifth month). The doctors gave me crappy drugs to stop the contractions and I left the hospital three days later.

I was so scared as I rubbed my growing belly, wondering how the hell I was going to pay for everything on top of all the medical concerns for myself and the baby. I kept praying to God to let something happen that would ease my stress.

As the months went on, my body was changing so drastically that I didn't even recognize myself in the mirror. Looking at my naked ass could have been one of the most scarring visuals in my life. No, I take that back—1970s ape pussy still beats it. But my ass got so big it didn't even have a crack anymore. It was just a giant tub of cottage cheese.

I not only felt horrific and looked horrific, but my low self-esteem from not being able to provide for my baby was killing me. It was during one good belly cry in the shower that I remembered to try to get myself back to satellite radio. I knew epiphanies happened on satellite radio, and I was determined to get there.

I waddled my alien body back to the Psychic Eye Book Shop and tried to energetically connect to the one that would help me. As I looked around, I was so grateful to be surrounded by such inspirational books. It was the first time I experienced gratitude for the gift that these authors bring to the world. Life gives us so many crazy personal experiences to go through, and by reading their experiences, I realized it could possibly save me from future bad ones if I applied their words of wisdom to my own life.

As I stood there holding on to four books, I giggled at a thought I had: "Wouldn't it be crazy if *I* wrote a book someday?"

When these questions pop into our conscious thoughts, wouldn't it be awesome to follow them with a question like "Why not?" Instead, my ego immediately shut it down. "Idiot, you type with one finger and failed English. Shut up, fool."

When I got home, I dove into the books, absorbing the words like the chocolate brownies I gorged on every night during pregnancy. I was finally back. I was awake. I was a happy, fat pregnant girl on satellite radio. There was no stress anymore. I realized everything that happened was for the best reason possible and the universe always figures out a way to help you get by. I knew the key was to surrender my worries and carry on with my pregnancy with the excitement a pregnant woman should have.

By the time I checked in to the hospital to deliver, I weighed 211 pounds. I was hoping to deliver a forty-pound baby, but no such luck. Evan was only six pounds.

The only way to describe the moment Evan was put in my arms is absolute heaven. I felt my heart physically grow another chamber. Evan was born on May 18, 2002. I also claim it as my birthday because my life began that day as well. I knew I was entering a phase in my life where my mission was to be the best mother I could possibly be to this little boy. I wasn't going to let him down.

About a month after delivery, I was sitting on the couch cuddling my baby when I started to reflect on all the crazy things that my body went through during pregnancy. I couldn't believe that even though I had read every pregnancy book on the market, not one was brutally honest. I mean *really* honest. I opened up my computer to make a list of shit no one warned me about in pregnancy. Then I would show it to my doctor so he could better inform women of what was about to happen to them.

As I clicked away with one finger on my keyboard, I flashed to the thought I had in the bookstore: "What if *I* wrote a book someday?" This time the voice was louder than my ego, but it wasn't quite loud enough for me to really believe I could. Instead I told myself, "Why don't you just pretend you're writing an email to Laura [my BFF] and share with her the funny, crazy moments in pregnancy?"

With Evan at my side, I spent ten hours a day clicking away with one finger on the keyboard and my other hand feeding Evan. I felt a rush of excitement that I was sharing information, just like all those authors I have read over the years.

When I finally finished, I printed it out and stared at it. I had never written anything in my life. I even paid people in college to write my papers for me. This accomplishment felt really good.

I sent the book to my acting agent, who sent it to my agency's literary department, and waited anxiously for a response. I knew that if they liked it, I wasn't a complete asshole for thinking I could do it.

A week later my agent called and said they turned it down. It was too crude.

Normally, this kind of news would force me to bed and I would curl up and cry for twenty-four hours. Instead, I listened to my inner voice. It said, "There are a lot more agents in the world than this one."

With that, I mailed my book to every book agent and publisher on the East Coast, just like every other person trying to catch a break. I was still unsure about where money would be coming from, but I knew that any effort put forth would send a signal to the universe that I wasn't fucking around.

I wanted to work.

Within a couple of months I was turned down by every literary agency in New York City. It reminded me of the time back in Chicago when I sent my photos to every modeling agency and they all turned me down. That flashback gave me the strength to keep hoping that something from somewhere would guide me toward my next move.

The next month I received a call from my lawyer telling me that a small boutique publishing company out of Boston was interested in my book. I couldn't believe that somebody other than my own mom believed in me. We quickly made a deal and they told me we would launch in a year. That seemed so far away. I needed the money *now*, not a year from now.

"Will I get an upfront fee?" I asked with a squeak of desperation.

"Not much, because you need to prove yourself as an author."

I wasn't going to argue. It seemed logical. With that, I decided to get my ass in shape and continue to act and host in La La Land doing odd jobs.

When it was time to finally promote the book, I had actually forgotten about it. I didn't really have high expectations. I just hoped that people who bought it would giggle and find entertainment in what I went through. *Live with Regis and Kelly* was the only big national show that agreed to have me come on to promote it, and I was beyond grateful. I flew to New York and giggled that I was there as an author!

I did the show, flew back home, and enjoyed reliving the hilarious symptoms of pregnancy now that they were way behind me. As I sat on the ground playing with Evan, I felt proud for the first time in my life. I gave birth to the most beautiful thing on Earth, *and* I wrote a book.

My thoughts then drifted and I giggled as I heard yet another question pop up in my head: "Wouldn't it be great if *Belly Laughs* became a best seller and you wrote more books?" This time my ego was louder and said, "Idiot, you're lucky the first one was published."

The next day the phone rang. It was my agent.

"Congratulations. You're a *New York Times* bestselling author. *Belly Laughs* is number seven on the list."

I screamed so loud that I think I broke my agent's eardrums and caused Evan to cry. I couldn't believe it. I was excited that this meant I could take yet another new direction in my career and morph into a mother who speaks her mind and tells the truth. I had no idea how, seven books later, putting that intention out there would have led to exactly that.

I followed *Belly Laughs* with *Baby Laughs*; *Life Laughs*; *Louder Than Words*; *Mother Warriors*; *Healing and Preventing Autism*; *Love, Lust & Faking It*; and now this here masterpiece, *Bad Habits*.

Not bad for a girl who failed English and types with one finger. Whoop, whoop!

me, turning my intentions
into reality

✣

26

Aho Mitakuye Oyasin

As my journey of enlightenment continued, I came across a group of friends who told me about an Indian sweat lodge they went to every Monday.

Not a pretend sweat lodge but a real, almost-die-in-it sweat lodge.

They told me how you go into the teepee to suffer so you don't have to suffer in the real world. Considering the amount of suffering I had been through as a Catholic, I didn't think that this experience would be nearly as bad, so I said, "Can you take me with you next time?"

I was told I was not allowed to go to the ceremony if I was having my period. (This was different from my boyfriend's tact at the time, which demanded that I throw down a black towel because he liked to battle with a red sword.) The explanation for the lodge's rule came later. Apparently, women have many very powerful spirit guides with them when they have their period. They help us get our bodily shit done, and they usually make us feel overly powerful, so that we finally can tell people how we really feel during PMS.

The modern term is called "being a bitch" but the Indians call it "being in your power." I liked the sound of their beliefs immediately.

When I arrived, I pulled up to the lodge and walked up to the Indian chief, named Chief. I offered him tobacco and asked if I could join the sweat lodge ceremony. He welcomed me and explained the rules that must be followed. I must obey the "moon time" rule, which was the no-period rule. He also stated that we must bless ourselves with sage smoke before we enter and say, "*Aho Mitakuye Oyasin.*"

"What does that mean?" I asked.

"It means 'to all my relations!'" he said.

"Sorry, I still don't understand," I said, being the curious asshole who has to question everything that I am.

"It means honoring all who are related, which is all of us. We are all connected."

"That's beautiful," I said while still trying to wrap my head around interconnectedness, which all of my spiritual books talked about.

Chief then said, "It is very important that you do not lift the bottom of the teepee and let air inside. We are in there for three hours and it will be very hot. You must pray through it."

"Why is that?" I asked.

"Because opening the bottom of the teepee will let evil spirits in," he said with strong authority.

That's all he needed to say. I was sure Ben or dead man holding his baby were still following me, and those bastards were not coming into my teepee.

I crawled inside the teepee, which probably should have held around thirty people comfortably. I counted fifty-five people going inside.

Once inside, I was told to crawl and tuck myself into a ball as close as possible to the person sitting next to me. Then another person sandwiched me in on the other side.

Once the teepee was filled with bodies, I realized I couldn't move. It was like being buried alive.

Chief entered last.

He pulled hot stones out of the fire and proceeded to pour water on them. Hot steam filled the teepee. Chief began to sing Indian chant songs and beat a drum.

I couldn't see anything and I couldn't move.

All I could think was, *Holy shitballs, I have to stay in here for three hours!*

Time moved at an excruciatingly slow pace. I compared it to a bad experience at hot yoga to get myself through it. I wasn't tolerating the heat very well and I needed a distraction. I wanted to talk to anyone around me who was willing to listen and get me through the ceremony. The guy I was next to seemed so relaxed and at peace. I had to ask him what his secret was.

He then told me that he gets inspired by his feces. He peers into the toilet and reads his stool like tea leaves.

Yes, I met a real-life shape-shitter.

I shook my head and tried to bring myself back to the present. Out of the yoga class. Back into the teepee. Another dimension of Hell.

My heart started to beat with the rhythm of the drum, which started to go faster and faster.

Then Chief poured more water on the stones, causing the temperature to get to at least 175 degrees. My face felt like it was melting off and I didn't know what to do with the huge amount of pain I was in.

I tried singing along with Chief.

"Hiyayayayayaya," I sang, but it wasn't working.

I dug my fist into the dirt I was sitting on and brought it up to my face so I could smear the dirt on it. I thought the mud might cool my skin. Instead, I just had a muddy face that was melting off.

Then Chief poured more water on the hot rocks. More steam filled the teepee. You could hear moans as if people were burning in Hell. I started to have a panic attack. I was freaking the hell out.

"Excuse me, Chief."

Chief stopped mid-song.

"You can interrupt only if it's an extreme emergency. You must work through the panic attack. If you work through it, you will have moved past a part of you that needed to go and will never come back. Be strong. You can do it."

How the hell did he know I was having a panic attack?

I had no idea how to calm myself down. My body was screaming at me to cool it off.

So I was left with no other choice but to come up with a sneaky plan.

I dug my index finger through the mud and poked it out the teepee. I only got one inch of my finger out, but the breeze on the tip of my finger was enough to calm me down.

About two minutes later, people started moaning strangely and then I heard the sound of vomiting. *Oh my God*, I thought, *that better not be the person next to me.*

Chief stopped his singing and spoke.

"Someone is letting evil spirits into the tent. People are getting sick. Who is doing this?"

Damn it, I thought. *What the hell do I do?*

I sat there waiting for someone else to admit to the demon entry, but no one did. So I did what any other wise person would do and stayed silent.

Chief then spoke again.

"Please understand that this is a very important part of the ceremony and you must not lift any part of the tent. We are all counting on each other to respect this."

Then Chief started singing again.

I felt bad about my finger poke, but it was like taking a sip of water after being in Death Valley for a week. I had to do it in order to survive.

As the third hour rolled around, I started to hallucinate. I think I was detoxing all the drugs I'd ever done in the past. I started seeing pink doughnuts singing songs to me in front of my face. Then I saw a leprechaun, with whom I had a full, audible conversation.

I finally realized that I had to poke my finger outside the teepee one more time in order to push through.

Ahhhhhhh, relief.

My index finger felt like it had won the lotto. I don't think any of my other nine fingers have forgiven me to this day.

Then, just when I thought I had gotten away with murder, I felt my finger getting crushed outside the teepee by a three-hundred-pound man in steel boots. I knew the fire keeper patrolling the teepee had just busted me. I couldn't scream because then everyone would know that I was the opener of the evil spirits.

Now my body was burning alive inside the teepee and my finger was being crushed to pieces outside the teepee.

If Hell on Earth exists, I had put myself in it here.

I finally managed to squirm my finger away from his boot and close the teepee back up.

As I sat there in the home stretch, I was amazed to realize that I had overcome my fear of evil spirits. To me, that was growth. Sure, I jeopardized the ceremony and possibly fucked some people up, but not caring about evil spirits was a huge accomplishment.

The ceremony was finally over. When I crawled out, it felt like I was being born again.

The cool air hitting my muddy face and the sound of the fire crackling were all so beautiful.

I sat down and felt good that I had managed to at least get through the ordeal . . . even if I cheated a little.

After reading about this experience, one would think that I would never go back to the lodge again. But no, not Jenny! Yes, that's right. I went back every Monday for ten years (except during moon time). I went for so many years because I was still under the belief that you need to suffer in order to be a good person.

It was only once I began to question my need to suffer, and subsequently couldn't come up with an answer, that I finally stopped going. I thought I would attempt something new in my life—the state of grace.

I no longer needed to feel pain in order to reach enlightenment. I was on a new path, and I was so grateful to my Indian lodge for teaching me this.

Aho Mitakuye Oyasin!!

✛

27

Curious Jenny and the
Man in the Big White Hat

To my mother and most other Catholics, the Vatican is to us what the Wailing Wall is to the Jews. Holy, holy! And for Catholics it doesn't get much holier than the pope's crib.

Growing up, my mother would have us turn on the TV to watch the pope say Mass from the Vatican, and I remember thinking how it looked like the most beautiful palace. Except there were no princes or princesses there, just really, really old people.

My mother was in love with the pope. Especially Pope John Paul II because he was also Polish.

When I was nine, I asked my mom how the pope was chosen.

She always had the best response: "By God."

How can anyone counter that?

Anything that had to do with anything was by God.

"Mom, how do miracles happen?"

"They are chosen by the grace of God."

"Mom, who picks the president of the United States?"

"God."

"Mom, why does it rain?"

"God is crying."

"Mom, why didn't the milkman come today?"

"God didn't want him to."

Boom, end of story.

So, being that the pope was like God's wingman on Earth like Robin is to Batman, my mom felt compelled to buy all the necessary pope merchandise she could get her holy hands on. It was damn near intervention time.

She had a collection of pope votive candles, pope air fresheners, pope travel cups, pope party plates, and even pope soap-on-a-rope. In 2009, the Vatican said no more to these trinkets in order to protect the papal brand. They claimed that the sale of pope paraphernalia was sacrilegious. In other words, they were missing out on the serious cash crop it could have brought in. The Church must have finally realized it should have seized the sales years ago and trademarked the pope like the Jolly Green Giant.

When I was six, there was an announcement that the pope was coming to Chicago. My mom went out of her mind with excitement. The whole neighborhood was shaken up.

Leading up to his arrival, my mom was crossing days off the calendar like it was her wedding date.

I remember the day he came quite clearly because my mom suddenly had no qualms about leaving us with a babysitter. She never got us a babysitter. She was always home. Looking back now, I appreciate that, but once I got to the teenage years, I couldn't have wanted her more gone from the house.

But the day the pope came, off she went in her big blue parka and her hair perfectly set, leaving her four girls with the babysitter.

I sat home sad because I missed her. Our babysitter did what most sitters did best and turned the TV on for us.

There, on the television, was the pope live from Chicago. He kept blessing the crowd, and all these baby boomers screamed as if he were a Beatle. The camera panned to a group of crazed women crying and waving their arms wildly, and lo and behold, there was my mother. In all of her glory, she was blowing kisses to the pope and jumping up and down. I couldn't believe out of a million crazed people, they showed my mom on TV! All I could think was that I really hoped Janet Baruch was watching. As you know, we didn't have a VCR back in the day, so my mom had to take my word for it that I saw her geek out on the pope.

F ast-forward. I'm now twenty-three.

I had to go to Italy to promote a new pair of sunglasses some Italian designer was launching. When I was told the gig was in Rome, I nearly crapped myself. That's where the Vatican is!

Anyway, upon my arrival, I was greeted by beautiful Italian men dripping with sex. I wished I didn't have a boyfriend at the time because I would have totally *Jersey Shore*'d it with every hot guy I saw.

The night I arrived, I was invited to dinner with the sunglasses designer. I didn't want to go by myself, so I asked if I could bring my wardrobe stylist and my makeup girl. They were both really close friends of mine and I pretty much traveled the world with them. After a few bottles of wine, I began playing footsie with a hot guy under the table.

Then I overheard someone at the table start talking about the Vatican.

I put my foot back inside my shoe and spoke up.

"My mom is the pope's number one fan. Have any of you guys ever met the pope?"

One of the Mafia-looking men said, "*Si!*"

Then the misogynistic guy next to him said, "We know people. That's what Italy is all about. Connections." He said this so matter-of-factly as he picked at his teeth with a business card.

Then, in all seriousness, I asked, "Do you think you can get the pope's autograph for me?"

The entire table burst into laughter. It was a scene straight out of a sitcom where the dumb blonde asks a question and everyone laughs their asses off, leaving the dumb blonde scratching her head. I felt like Julia Roberts in *Pretty Woman* when she's sitting with a group of upper-crust businessmen and is confused by the forks.

"I don't get why that's funny," I said.

Again, the table exploded into uproarious laughter. The misogynistic guy was checking me out from head to toe. He was totally jealous of my outfit and it added to his holier-than-thou behavior.

"Well, you said you were connected, so I was just looking to get something for my mom."

One of the Mafia-looking guys said to me, "Pope's not gonna sign an autograph, but I can do something else for ya, if you don't tell anyone."

"Of course not."

(Although, here I am about to write it all in a book. Note to the reader: Don't ever tell me a secret.)

The Mafia guy looked at his watch, which said it was about midnight, and then looked at me with a grin.

"I can take you to the Vatican right now and take you to see the pope's apartment, where no one gets to go. He's out of town, so we can sneak you in."

"*Oh my gawwwddd!!!* My mom is gonna shit when I tell her!"

"We just told you not to tell anyone."

"Oh yeah. Oops."

Mafia man looked at my girlfriends and said, "You guys want to come too?"

I could tell my friends did not want to go. They were exhausted from the flight. Plus, they were Jewish.

Of course they wanted no part of this, but I gave them the stare of death so that they would join me in one of the most amazing invitations a mere mortal could get on Earth.

"They are Catholic too. Of course they want to come," I blurted out.

"Yay," my friend Alyssa responded.

Then Andrea, my even more Jewish friend, said, "Sure. I love the pope."

What good friends I have!

Off we went, shoved into the backseat of a little town car, zipping through the streets of Rome at midnight. My tummy had butterflies with the anticipation of being in a place that was basically the Holy Grail.

First, the car pulled into the front of the Vatican to give me a peek out the window. It was the palace I saw on TV when I was a little girl! Stunning.

My mouth hung open as I looked at all the statues of saints on pillars that surrounded the Vatican. I used to pray to all of these saints with JoJo.

This was an amazing moment for me, but it was quickly ruined by my Jewish friend Alyssa, who said, "Why do they have all these gargoyles around the Vatican?"

I kicked her in the shin as hard as I could.

"Those are all the saints, you idiot. You should really have worn your glasses."

Moments later, we pulled up to the gate. It was spooky. It reminded me of going into my scary basement with JoJo. The guards looked more like Mason cult leaders than Palace Keepers. Had this not been the Vatican, I would have gotten out of the car and run for my life.

Then our car slowly crept in and we drove to the back of the church. A man came out to greet us who resembled Igor, Frankenstein's assistant. Except this Igor spoke in Italian.

The men I was with began to go back and forth in conversation and kept pointing at me. In any other situation, I might have flashed my boobs to gain entry into a place, but here I think I would have been struck by lightning.

"*Sì*," said Holy Igor, and we walked past him.

We did it. The Mafia men opened a door and we were inside. No one was in sight. The door we went through seemed more like an employee entrance, but that all changed when we opened door number three.

Remember when Charlie from *Willy Wonka & the Chocolate*

Factory opened the door to the chocolate river candy room for the first time? How his eyes took everything in?

That was me.

The room we stood in looked like a secret cathedral unto its own. There were high ceilings with Michelangelo-like paintings on them. The faint, familiar scent of frankincense tickled my nostrils. The most interesting part was that each corner of the room had enormous wooden doors. They weren't just any doors. They looked as if each one was meant to take you to a different part of Heaven.

"Where do these doors lead to?" I asked. "They look so important."

Mafia man said, "You are standing in the room that adjoins the Vatican, St. Peter's, the Sistine Chapel, and the pope's apartment. It is the center that no visitors get to see. Clergymen can easily access where they want to go by opening that specific door."

It really was an amazing sight.

It was just like being in a dream where someone says, "Choose the door to your new life."

Even my Jews were amazed by the creativity of the architect who was able to have all these structures meet up in one room. But just when I thought this couldn't be more awesome, one of my Jews put her foot in her mouth.

Pointing to a painting of Jesus, she asked: "Who is that?"

Nooooo!!! was all I could think. I could see the Mafia men look at each other strangely. I wasn't going to let this stop me from living a dream of my mother's, so I started laughing with a loud cackle.

"You are so funny, Alyssa. Hahahahahaha." My voice echoed louder than I've ever heard it before.

I was the only one laughing, but it was the only thing I could think of to cover the embarrassment.

Mafia man then pointed to one of the doors in the corner of the room.

"Through that door is the pope's apartment. Ready to see it?"

I wish I could have done cartwheels all the way up to the door, but instead I shouted, "*Sì! Sì! Sì!!*"

With his permission, I opened the door and holy aioli! My eyes had never seen a hallway like this. Marble, gold, and cherubs hanging off the ceiling.

It was absolutely spectacular.

As I continued to walk, I started to take in how much money was around me. These weren't cherubs from Target, if you know what I'm saying. Thoughts of cracking one off and feeding a starving nation crossed my mind.

"Psst. Come here."

Mafia man then brought us down a hallway and we entered a closet.

Holy Stromboli, this is the pope's closet! I was surrounded by all of the pope's robes. Needless to say, there were a lot of them.

I looked at my friends and whispered, "Isn't this amazing?"

They whispered back, "Not really."

Mafia man then said, "Come here, Jenny."

"Don't. He might be trying to kill you," Andrea said.

"What is wrong with you guys?" I said. "We are in the Vatican! People don't get murdered here. Relax."

I walked over to Mafia man, who led me to the mirror. He then put on top of my head . . . wait for it . . . the pope's freaking hat! That's right! That tall, giant hat he always wears was sitting on top of this Playboy Playmate's head.

I couldn't believe my eyes.

I stared at myself in the mirror in awe. It was totally insane.

I mean, come on.

Can you even imagine what the nuns at school would think?

I turned around to show my Jews.

"Look, you guys. How insane is this? I'm wearing the pope's hat!"

I couldn't contain my childlike excitement, so I started bopping around in an impromptu Teletubbies-style dance.

They both responded with a monotone "Wow."

Alyssa was carelessly chewing on a KitKat bar, so I smacked it right out of her hand.

"What the hell are you doing? You can't eat in here."

I carefully took off the pope's hat and thanked Mafia man immensely. Then I spotted the most beautiful selection of crucifixes. To say "beautiful crucifix" sounds like an oxymoron, but if these were for sale, the Kardashians would certainly have one in their home.

I brought my Jews with me to take a closer look to try to get them involved in some way.

I held one beautiful cross up and said, "My mother would absolutely lose her mind if she saw this crucifix."

Andrea whispered, "Do you want me to put it in my purse?"

"Are you out of your freaking mind? No! What's wrong with you guys? We're almost done. Just be cool."

Mafia man said, "Let's go to one more spot."

We entered a new room that was small and gold. And by gold, I mean GOLD.

In the center of the room was an elevator. This was no ordinary elevator. This is the kind of elevator that a king or queen would take to Heaven if they died. It was ornate and a tad bit scary.

Speaking of scary, Holy Igor had now joined our tour.

Again, the men started talking to one another in Italian and all I could do was smile and nod.

While they were going back and forth, I decided to check in with my Jews, whom I could hear giggling.

"What's going on? Why are you laughing?"

"We don't know what's wrong, but we have the giggles."

Oh no! They had caught a case of the church giggles.

Alyssa said, "We kind of feel like we are going to be murdered any second now and we can't stop laughing."

Their shoulders bobbed up and down as they launched into a fit of hysteria. Sweat dripped down my face. I was about to have a heart attack.

"Stop it," I commanded.

Their shoulders kept bobbing. Squeaky noises held in a volcanic eruption of laughter.

"Shut. The. Fuck. Up." I mouthed it to them slowly with daggers in my eyes.

That one seemed to knock some sense into them. They could tell I was pissed.

"Do not screw this up or I will murder you myself."

Holy Igor then proceeded to unlock a drawer that had a key

inside. He held it up like it was the key to the room holding the Ten Commandments.

"Danananananana," Holy Igor said in Italian, which I'm guessing meant "Here's the key!"

Mafia man said, "He's going to let us take a ride in the elevator. It takes the pope to do Mass in the Vatican. After he changes, he comes in here and rides the elevator to the church."

"I'm not going in that thing," Alyssa said.

"Yes, you are," I said.

"No, I'm not."

"Yes, you are. You are going to fucking do it," I whispered into her ear like a gremlin.

Mafia man said, "I know it looks scary, but that's because it's one hundred years old."

"Now I'm definitely not going in it," Alyssa said.

"Yes, you are," I said, gritting my teeth.

"No, I'm not."

Then Mafia man, in a calming voice, said, "Trust me, it's okay."

We all entered the elevator. It was a snug fit and tension was in the air.

Then my worst fear happened. No, we didn't get stuck.

My Jews lost control of their church giggles and started busting out laughing to the point of losing oxygen. I'm glad they weren't wearing a skirt like I was because I didn't want to witness any pee trickles that were happening. They were half on the ground and half standing, holding their stomachs and laughing their asses off.

This is where the pope preps to come out and do a big, holy Mass, and my Jews were losing their shit.

I was totally and completely dying. I tried stepping on their toes as hard as I could, but nothing would stop them—not even the stabbing of my stiletto heels was knocking sense into them.

"What's going on?" Mafia man asked.

"They have a fear of elevators and, you know, it's like gallows humor."

"Okay, well, let's go back down," Mafia man said. "I don't want them to be scared."

Damn them! I couldn't believe it.

The elevator started to head back down.

Finally, the girls started to get their giggles under control, but then Alyssa all of a sudden got the bright idea to come out and say she's a Jew.

"We should really tell you something. Andrea and I are—"

I interrupted and shouted, "They are so excited to be here!"

Not that there was anything wrong with saying they were Jewish, but I had lied about them being Catholic. I didn't want to get ratted out. The elevator door opened to Holy Igor standing there with a big, creepy smile as he started to speak Italian again.

Mafia man translated: "He has some holy water blessed by the pope that we could dip our finger in and make the sign of the cross."

Shit, shitballs, shit-o-rama, I thought, because I knew two things: my Jews didn't know how to make the sign of the cross and they were about to blow my cover.

Holy Igor approached Alyssa and said, "Nanananana," which I think meant "Go ahead and have some holy water."

Alyssa backed away as if the water were going to melt her. "No thanks." Holy Igor looked confused and started moving closer to her.

Alyssa shouted, "I said no thanks, weirdo!"

Then Andrea rescued her by announcing, "We're Jewish! We don't want any! Oh my gawd!"

The car ride home was pretty quiet. I was never hired again by the Italian designers and now you know why.

When we got back to the room, I laid into my friends. They apologized profusely, but they explained how scary and weird it was for them. They went on to tell me that they were thinking about me and how special this would be for my mom, so they brought me a souvenir to give to her.

I gasped as they pulled out the crucifix from the pope's closet.

28

Step Away from the Vicodin and Sit on the Toilet

Most of Los Angeles is guilty of enjoying a Vicodin without having a painful ailment. What people who have not taken it before don't realize is that it also heals emotional ailments for about four hours.

Sorry. "Heal" is the wrong word.

Vicodin numbs emotional aliments for about four hours. Unless you take two. Then your emotional pain will be numbed for eight hours.

I wasn't aware of this oasis away from emotional hurt until an LA troll said, "Want to party with some Vicodin?"

"Party with Vicodin?" I asked.

"Yeah," the troll said. "Take one and just get creamy. You can have a beer and make it even better."

"Okay!" I exclaimed. I swallowed a Vicodin and immediately felt all of my muscles relax. I felt so happy, so peaceful. I didn't have a care in the world. This was the best idea ever.

I couldn't believe I wasted so many years tripping my balls off on hallucinogenic drugs. This shit rocked.

Or so I thought.

I then chased it down with a beer and became violently ill. I spent the entire night barfing in a stall next to a hen party of girls who were either peeing or snorting or both simultaneously.

I was so scared; I thought I was going to die. I was so mad at myself for trusting a troll I didn't even know. That night I must have had two devils on one shoulder high-fiving each other.

Well, I never mixed the two again. But because the drug is so yummy—better known as addictive—anytime I heard even the mention of someone having tooth surgery or back pain, I would bodycheck anyone in my way to ask, "Got Vicodin?"

Then, just like clockwork, the universe delivered Vicodin to me on a truck.

I threw my back out and tore ligaments from my mid-back to my neck. I laid in bed for three months.

I could barely move.

I don't think I ever slept in those entire three months. I was taking Vicodin every three hours, twenty-four hours a day, and was still in excruciating pain. The drug eventually made me incredibly depressed, and I experienced the worst constipation of my life.

Because I couldn't walk, going to the bathroom was a trip I would make only once a day. It was like trying to give birth, and if I was lucky, I would conceive a piece of shit that was the size of the queen bee of Nerds candy. It's like a gremlin grabbing hold of your asshole but from the inside.

I would sit on the toilet screaming, trying to get the Vicodin pebble out of my butt. It took an hour to squeeze out one pebble.

I had heard about people who were taking forty Vicodin a day. There is no way those people were shitting giggles, bricks, or anything for that matter. I went twice in two weeks and shit a grand total of four pebbles.

When my back finally recovered, I had to detox all the Vicodin I had. I had never experienced a detox other than in the sweat lodge teepee, and going off Vicodin was one of the most painful physical experiences I had ever gone through. My legs cramped. I was dripping in sweat, while also freezing.

And I was depressed. I couldn't wait to get past it and poop like a normal human being again.

After about a week, I finally felt like old Jenny.

Sadly, that was the problem—old Jenny. I realized that being numb for three months put my spiritual growth on hold. When you don't feel, you don't heal.

Coming back to reality after an emotional hiatus is really tough. Usually in life, you take things as they come, deal with them, and then move on. But even just a three-month hiatus of not feeling anything made my reentry miserable.

Feeling uncomfortable emotionally was no fun. It sucked. Having an oasis once in a while from feeling bad felt really good.

For example, my agent calls and I didn't get a part. So I'll go on a shopping spree. Two weeks later, my boyfriend is fighting with me, so I'll have a drink. The next weekend, I feel worthless in the world, so I'll stuff my face with McDonald's. This behavior is so easily understood by all of us, I'm sure. But I wanted to figure out a way to take a few of those moments and replace them with a new coping method.

The problem was that I had to teach it to myself. One thing they don't teach in school or church is coping skills.

When I talked to my sister JoJo about the emotions that stirred up in my chest that made me want to find something to numb it, she described it as "the rash is back." She said she could be driving in her car singing a great song and all of a sudden the rash creeps up, and she says, "Hello, asshole. There you are. I feel you." I asked her what she did about it besides try to make it go away as fast as possible.

She replied, "I try to sit on the toilet and feel it."

"Why do you need to sit on the toilet?"

"Because it's the only place where I can truly let it all hang out and relax. And then I allow myself to feel the pain. Sometimes I have no idea what it is, but I learned that sometimes you don't need to attach a thought to it. Just feel it. Just sit in it. And when it moves past you, like a storm, the other side is rainbows."

"Or a big deuce in the toilet."

"Shut up."

The next time I experienced the pain rash, I immediately tried to figure out how to numb it.

Then I remembered JoJo's new coping skill.

As I walked to the bathroom to give it a try, I heard voices in my head saying, "Why the hell do you want to feel this emotional garbage? It's going to suck. Go take a pill, go get a drink, go order a pizza, but don't feel it."

I told the voice—which I later learned was ego—to shut the hell up. I pulled my pants down, sat on the toilet, and let it all hang out.

Waves of the pain in my soul emerged. I accepted it. I didn't fight it. I didn't even think about why it was there. I just felt it. Even though it wasn't pleasant, it felt right. It felt like I was going through an emotional car wash.

It took only about forty-five minutes and a couple of noxious farts, and I felt like the worst was behind me. I walked out of the bathroom feeling as if I went from fifth grade to seventh grade.

Holy shart.

I realized in that moment that by numbing, I was just hitting the pause button on spiritual growth, and that if you don't face your shit here and there, your life will quickly turn into shit. I was grateful that JoJo gave me this great new coping skill, but what was coming up next in my life made the pain rash look like nothing in comparison.

There was no toilet big enough.

me, praying you love this book

✳

29

Losing My Identity

I 'm sorry. Your son has autism."

I felt my soul being torn out of my body. I felt betrayed by God. I was angry, sad, and beyond scared.

All of my memories of my perfect little baby were being stomped on when the doctor gave me this diagnosis.

How could this happen?

Why would God make this happen? If God is good, why would He/She/It do this to people?

The doctor didn't give me a glimmer of hope and told me to just accept it.

He wasn't the only one.

Every doctor I bombarded with questions told me a similar story. It reminded me of my Catholic school days in religion class where I was not encouraged to dig for more answers. Just accept it. I did, but I came to realize that acceptance doesn't mean giving up. If I had to go to Hell and back to save my boy, that's exactly what I was going to do.

Reading bedtime stories was always a special time for Evan and me. I saw the enchantment in his eyes with every page I turned. I was as much in awe of him as he was with the story I was telling. He wanted to learn and take everything in like every other thriving child.

I promised I would do everything to give him the world to explore.

Weeks later, Evan had a seizure that was so horrific it put him into cardiac arrest. I was still waiting for the paramedics to arrive when he took his last breath and his eyes dilated. I dropped to my knees and stared at his lifeless body.

Words could never truly express what happened to me in this moment, but I did in fact have a conversation with God and I knew He/She/It was going to hear me this time.

"Bring him back. Bring him back." I placed my loving hand on his little chest. "Bring him back, God." Thoughts of being a mother who lost a child were unacceptable. I knew I would find the nearest exit to this life if I lost him. I wasn't strong enough. "Bring him back, God!"

I thought about how I wouldn't get to see this boy turn into a man. I wouldn't see him kiss his bride. I wouldn't hear him giggle anymore. All of these thoughts tormented me. "Bring him back, God! Bring him back!"

Then I heard a voice. I wondered if this was the same voice that the nuns heard.

It said, "Everything is going to be okay."

And with that, my body relaxed.

I described this in my other book, *Louder than Words*, as God's Valium.

The paramedics finally arrived and started CPR on Evan. They put him on the stretcher and, while carrying him to the ambulance, they continued to do CPR on him.

I was watching this unfold in front of me and all I kept hearing was "Everything is going to be okay." The voice was so powerful I couldn't even attempt to second-guess it. It was a fact, and my body was physiologically reacting to that.

I remained calm.

I got into the front seat of the ambulance and looked back, watching them continue to do CPR on him.

A few moments later, the paramedics stopped, looked up at me, and gave me a thumbs-up. God was right tonight. Everything was going to be okay.

I wish that feeling could have stayed with me on the nights I would scream and cry in my shower.

The pain of watching Evan suffer with autism was so incredibly horrific at times that it would cause my body to tremble. I remember thinking that if life is a roller coaster, this time in my life was the lowest part of my ride. All I knew was that "up" had to be coming soon.

How did I know?

I guess faith.

This was my true test of faith.

I finally understood what the nuns meant by having faith, because faith was the only hope I had of getting through this. It's what got me off the shower floor. It's what got me out of bed. It's what got me to keep going when all I wanted to do was medicate myself away from the hell of autism.

Being a single mom during this time was debilitating for me. I felt alone and scared. I would pray to God for stupid jobs to come in to help pay for everything Evan needed.

I witnessed miracles after I pleaded to God for help.

"I need help with speech therapy, God." Boom bam, I would get a cheesy commercial. I was never so grateful to sell out during this time in my life.

I often reflect on why autism happened to me. I once had a person tell me that Satan was the one responsible, not God. This person insisted that God would do no such thing. I don't believe that for a second.

I made a deal with God the day Evan was diagnosed: "You help me heal my boy; I'll teach the world how I did it."

And, with that, I will pay it forward the rest of my life by sharing my experience and helping this cause. It saddens me to imagine if I had listened to the doctor try to convince me to just succumb to autism without any expectations for improvement. The joy in seeing Evan continually progress is overwhelming as he opens doors I was told would stay closed.

About a year after the diagnosis, which also included a divorce, I felt the need to raise my frequency again. I knew I couldn't handle being on AM anymore.

I missed satellite radio. AM definitely served its purpose during this time, though.

On AM, I could pop a pill and make the sad day go away. On AM, I could blame everyone around me for my suffering. On AM, I was able to feel sorry for myself. But I knew that was all bullshit and that shifting out of AM would bring me the peace I was ready for.

I again started reading books that empowered me and brought me new insight. I knew that because I intended to spiritually shift higher, I would be drawn to the right books to help get me there.

I picked up *A New Earth* by Eckhart Tolle.

This was three years before Oprah Winfrey had him on her show. I just happened to stumble upon the book as it caught my eye on display in the new releases.

At first, I had trouble understanding the book. It was almost as if it were written in another language. But something inside of me said to keep going, keep reading.

The more I read, the more I shifted, and the words began to make sense.

The book was turning my dial, and eventually I hit satellite radio. I was buzzing. I was alive. I was awake again. One of the most amazing parts of the book was the recognition of my own pain body. This is exactly where I was with Evan's diagnosis and where many of us get stuck in spiritual evolution.

My pain body identified with feeling guilty for my son's autism. I identified with it being my fault. When I realized that and understood that it was my pain body and ego enjoying that guilt as if it were food, I was able to disconnect myself from the pain body and rise above it.

Even now, when I identify myself as this or that, the pain body easily rises up again within me and starts devouring the situation like an addiction. Sometimes I can almost hear it laugh when I find myself starting the Woe Is Me game with myself.

In case you're confused with identification, let me give you some examples you can relate to:

"I'm allowed to be a bitch because I had a horrible childhood."

"I'm allowed to be worried because I don't have any money."

These are all things that we identify with.

We then allow the pain body to run us like the aliens in *Invasion of the Body Snatchers*. If we can open our minds and realize we come from a place where none of that exists (let's call it "Heaven"), then we can realize that none of this is actually real. I know it sounds "out there" to some people, but when you spend many years on the floor of the Psychic Eye Book Shop, shit starts to click.

I had the opportunity to have dinner with Eckhart Tolle, and I asked him about my problem of not being able to stay on satellite radio.

He giggled and said something like, "When you spiritually evolve, it's normal to go in and out. You call it satellite radio. But the time being on AM starts to become less and less through the years until eventually you operate from satellite radio most of the time. You go up and down on a roller coaster until the roller coaster starts to go in a straight line."

And boy was I operating from satellite radio during this time.

My friends started calling me weird because when they would come over with a problem, I was able to immediately see them identifying with it.

I got taken advantage of financially pretty bad during this awakening, and I never even got upset for a second.

I watched it happen as if I were watching a TV show. If I had felt pain during that time, it would have meant I was identifying as a victim who got taken advantage of and would have kick-started my pain body to react.

I was the awareness behind my situation, watching it unfold, and it was fucking awesome!

My friend Laura from college called me and said she was heading out to Los Angeles for a visit and I had better not be going through one of my "phases."

I knew what she meant because I was knee-deep shit in my phase.

Again, I downshifted and brought myself back to AM. Again, I hoped that Eckhart Tolle was right and that I would be back on satellite radio sooner than last time.

me   Evan

30

Evan's Chapter

I was lying in bed next to Evan writing this book, and he asked if he could take my computer and write his own chapter.
Here it is:

This is Evan. My life is great. And I have a mom that is very

nice. I like to call my mom Fluffy because her clothes and hair are

always so fluffy. Oh, and I also love a two-legged elephant.

Love,

Evan

Recovering Catholic

A few years ago, I did a TV show pilot that had me interview a nun about Heaven and Hell.

I couldn't think of a better person in the world to interview. Woohoo!

I flew my mother out to Los Angeles to be there for the taping. I knew she would love to see me bring Hollywood and God together in any way possible. She wore her Sunday best church outfit and her hair was set perfectly, just like old times.

I started the segment by saying, "Sister Elizabeth, many people have their own perceptions of what Hell is like. Can you describe the scene a sinner might expect upon his or her arrival in Hell?"

"The Catholic Church has never stated anyone was ever in Hell," she replied very matter-of-factly.

"Excuse me?" I said with my mouth hanging open. My uterus fell into my vagina. "I think I misunderstood you," I said. "I thought I just heard you say no one is in Hell."

"That's right. We never made a statement about it."

A familiar voice shouted from the audience, "What the hell is she talking about?" My mother was shouting from the bleachers with her hands on her hips.

I composed myself and tried to channel my inner Diane Sawyer, but as soon as I was about to say something, I froze. I flashed back to all the moments the nuns taught me about Hell. I flashed back to the ninety million homilies from priests warning me about the wrath of Hell. I flashed back to when I was a little girl who used to think God was glorious and then also feared Him because He could send me to Hell!

This wasn't fair.

I wanted to cry.

I wanted to knock the table over.

I wanted to pull off the nun's habit, point my finger in her face, and call her another hypocrite in my life.

But I didn't.

I composed myself and spoke. "You can understand, Sister, that this statement seems out of nowhere considering many Catholics were taught that Hell is where you go if you commit a mortal sin and don't confess it."

"Theologians developed an image of Hell with punishment, but we have yet to prove that anyone is there."

I then heard JoJo. (She has been my makeup artist for the past fifteen years. Even though we live together, I'm grateful she doesn't crawl into my bed and pee on me anymore.) Anyway, I heard JoJo cough loudly in the audience in the tone of calling "bullshit."

I flashed her a secret sisters smirk. I felt compelled to suddenly fulfill my own personal vendetta against this nun, but I knew it wasn't the time or place.

I straightened up and tried to stick to the script.

I couldn't.

"Sister, so you are saying theologians made up an image of Hell with people burning in a pit of flames, and it's our fault for believing that image literally?"

"Well, yes. No one is in Hell."

On the outside I was completely calm.

On the inside I was reeling and tiring from my triple-decade mental crusade to uncover the truth.

Later that day, when I got home, I realized I had finally lost faith in religion. The contradictions, the guilt, the shame, my mom and dad believing they're going to Hell, the priest molestation cover-up; it all felt darn right dirty.

My new path of staying tuned in to satellite radio was what made me feel amazing and connected to the outside world as well as myself. I was empowered more than ever and compassionate toward others. I didn't want to be part of this contradictory religion anymore. I was beyond twelve steps into recovery.

32

Finding My State of Grace

After enduring twelve years of Catholic school; numerous life coaches, yogis, gurus, and astrologers; and hundreds of spiritual books and meetings with many different religious sectors, I've come to realize that we are all a little right and we are all a little wrong.

The most wonderful thing we have in common is faith.

When I invited the Mormons to come over to do a blessing on Evan after his seizure, I was so taken aback by the power of their faith. They didn't care that I told them I didn't want to become Mormon but I still wanted them to do this prayer for my son because I had heard it worked. They didn't bat an eye. I watched them put their hands on Evan and pray, and I was so moved by what moved them—their faith.

No matter what religion people choose to live by, I came to realize that their choice is ultimately what is best for them.

Who cares if someone prays to an elephant if that elephant puts them in a state of grace?

The holy wars are what get us into trouble. If people minded their own business as far as religion is concerned and didn't get caught up in saving other people's souls, they just might be able to save their own souls and bless those around them with their contagious state of euphoria.

Indeed, the world needs more love.

Today, I looked up at the sky like I used to do when I was a little girl. The sun was shining on me and I felt the warm breeze glide across my face. God feels glorious again . . . exactly how I felt when I was a little girl. No more fear of His wrath giving me a cold shoulder. Just warmth. Just love.

I am awake.

I'm on satellite radio. I'm not sure how long I'll stay on it—maybe a few months this time if I'm lucky. Unless, of course, someone has tooth surgery. Then I'm totally pooping a Vicodin pebble.

After reading this book, some people still might call me a sinner; shame me for my bad habits. I prefer to think of myself as an ambitious student thriving in this awesome school called "life." Thank you for sharing this journey with me.

ACKNOWLEDGMENTS

Kerri Kolen, my kickass editor: Thanks for being talented and cool and accepting my invitation to join me for some drinks in Hell after writing this book.

Jennifer Rudolph Walsh, my amazing book agent: Thanks for always having my back and for having bigger balls than Ari.

Bill Kempin, the *Kansas City Star* doesn't know how lucky they are. You are not only an amazing friend but one hell of a writer. Thanks for making me sound smarter and for being the most amazing fact-checker of Catholicism next to the pope. Your mom should be proud! Follow Bill *@BillKempin* or *www.billkempin.com*.

Danielle Alicia Skalnik, who knew Jesus was a comedian? Bitch, you are funny, talented, and need to be writing more. Thank you for the extra laughs you brought to this last supper. Bless you my child. Follow Danielle *@theatricalism*.

Kathleen McVey, thank you for finding my photos. Without you, there would be no proof that I existed as a child. Considering we both got letters from you know who . . . I'll see you in Hell too. Follow Kathleen *@kathleenthame*.

Follow me at
@JennyMcCarthy